THE PRACTICAL
GARDENING CALENDAR

THE PRACTICAL
GARDENING CALENDAR

A MONTH BY MONTH GUIDE

© Naumann & Göbel Verlagsgesellschaft mbH, a subsidiary of
VEMAG Verlags- und Medien Aktiengesellschaft, Cologne
www.apollo-intermedia.de

Complete production: Naumann & Göbel Verlagsgesellschaft mbH, Cologne
Printed in Poland

Contents

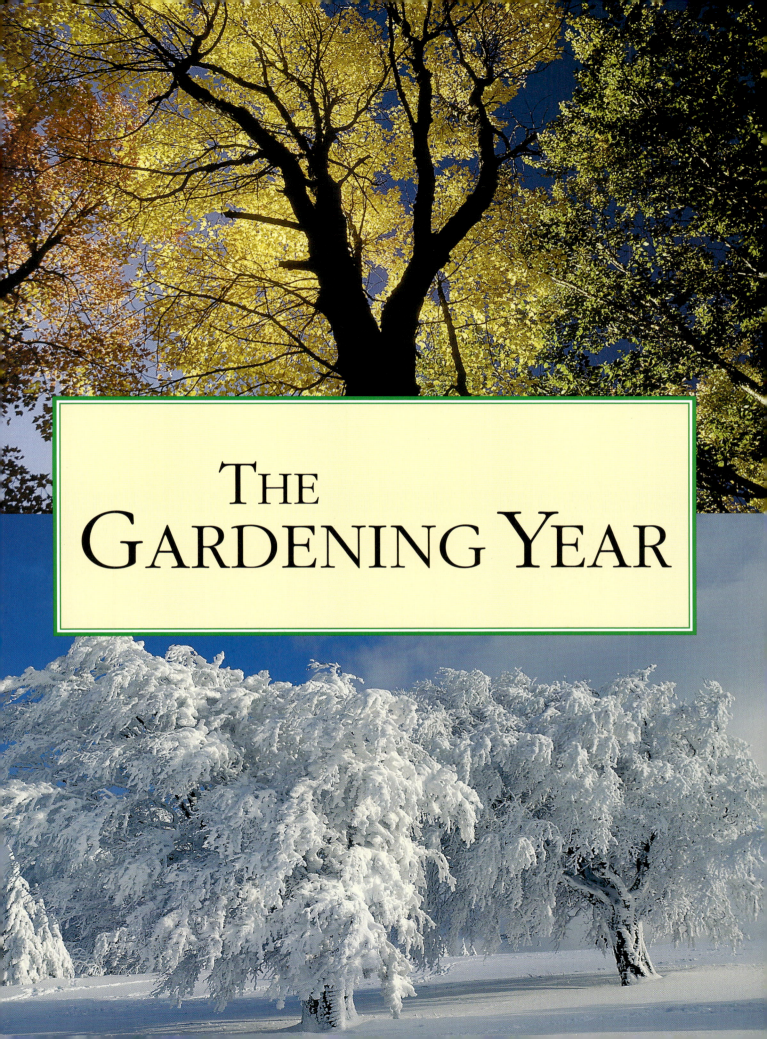

THE
GARDENING YEAR

A YEAR IN THE GARDEN

Whether you like a sea of blossom in spring and summer, a riot of colour from autumn leaves or frost and snow-covered trees in winter – the first thing any gardener comes to know is that there is a time and place for everything. There is no better way to learn the rules of nature than to garden, as it makes us feel so much a part of the changing seasons.

> Small herbs have grace; great weeds do grow apace.
>
> William Shakespeare, *King Richard the Third*

Show me your garden and I'll tell you who you are—to put a new twist on an old saying. Each gardener's handwriting on the land is unique. Soil and climate, budget and space will dictate some conditions, but what you make of them reflects your taste and attitude to nature. Your character is reflected in your style. There are many kinds of gardener: the fan of vibrant ornamentals, the would-be farmer with the biggest potatoes and pumpkins, and the tidy perfectionist who can't resist training trees along trellises or coaxing rows of perennials to salute one another in across the walk. These carica-tures don't exist in pure form, but inclinations in one direction or another are often discernible.

Sometimes choices are driven by the latest trend, as the gardening world certainly has its fads. But much of gardening taste can be roughly divided into English and French styles. At times the pendulum swings towards the strict horticultural school, rooted in Versailles and emphasising symmetry and line, then back again to a more natural look, however deliberately achieved. This finds its fullest expression in what many think of as the typical

English country garden. But anywhere people are involved, wilderness cannot prevail in its purest form, nor ruler and compass determine the final gardening outcome.

The most crucial factor in design is the purpose of a garden. It's easier to create a romantic look in a rockery or heather garden than in a vegetable plot. A pond lends itself more readily to the natural look than a bed of cut flowers, and the edges of a farmer's garden or an open field accommodate an abandon of wildflowers much better than the tiny, jewel-like front garden of a terraced house.

The personal taste of the garden's creator is decisive in any case, and won't be changed by critique. With the necessary skills and a bit of luck, your garden can become your own personal statement.

NATURE'S CALENDAR

Our 12-month calendar can't always tell us what to expect from nature in our gardens. It's not just that April is unpredictable—nature has its own rhythms that every gardener has to get to grips with before our efforts with spades and seeds can be crowned with success.

Astronomically determined dates for the start and end of the seasons are roughly accurate, as they correspond to the solstices and equinoxes that mark the earth's position in relation to the sun. But there are plenty of discrepancies! In spite of how a season ought to behave, sudden cold snaps, flooding, hail or heat waves can come as a surprise. It is advisable to adjust your gardening activity to the weather and regional conditions rather than any strict timeframes. As we know, gardeners just an hour or so south of us will have trees in flower before there is any sign of spring in the north.

Phenology, or the study of natural phenomena, achieves a more nuanced breakdown of the seasons through observation of plants. On the right is an example of such a plan, which emphasises what happens in the garden rather than following pre-determined monthly milestones. This book follows a month-by-month progression through the year for the purpose of organization; but bear in mind that it is only intended a guide, and take phenological factors into account when putting any gardening advice into practice.

Weather forecasts and your own observation of the weather are important in determining what garden tasks to take in hand when, as official forecasts are often broad and have only limited regional application. Ultimately, you are the best judge of how your garden's site (wind-prone, sheltered, sunny, high or low) and its plants will weather the seasons.

In this way every gardener is a phenologist of sorts. Careful observation of your garden's conditions can make a world of difference to your results. Though most plants quickly recover from a slow start in the growing season, frost or wind damaged plants will show distress for some time, for instance, if you plant them too early. Nature's clock certainly has its own way of ticking and it pays to simply go with the flow.

> In temperate climates the year is divided up according to the path of the sun – which is how the astronomically defined quarters or seasons of the year first came about. But nature knows no such strict boundaries. The phenological calendar is a more detailed description of seasonal changes. It is based on age-old observations of weather patterns, flowering sequences and other regularly occurring natural phenomena. Its divisions are somewhat different.

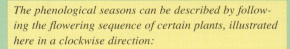

The phenological seasons can be described by following the flowering sequence of certain plants, illustrated here in a clockwise direction:

1.	Foretaste of spring	Snowdrops appear
2.	Early spring	Forsythias flower
3.	Height of spring	Apple blossom time
4.	Early summer	Cocksfoot in full bloom
5.	Height of summer	Grapevines flower
6.	Late summer	Barley is golden ripe
7.	Early autumn	'Naked ladies' flower
8.	Mid autumn	Acorns fall
9.	Late autumn	Leaves fall
10.	Winter	Virtual absence of any flowering plants

THE WEATHER

Hugely influential but sadly out of our control – nothing is as crucial to a gardener as the weather. Yet the weather can never keep all gardeners happy. What's good for some makes others groan, so it's important to take the weather just as it comes – adopting a relaxed attitude can make the difference between pleasant days in the garden and stressful ones.

Rain may generally put a dampener on things, but without rainfall there can be no growth in the natural world – no blossom and no harvest. And anyway, a summer rain shower is often followed by a delightful rainbow that more than makes up for the deluge.

Wind exerts a mechanical effect over plants and, depending on the strength of the wind, can bend them, blow them over or even uproot them. Unfavourable wind tunnels created by nearby obstacles can sometimes increase the potential for damage. Wind also has a drying effect, even without the added impact of any sunshine. Mulch layers can help to counteract this.

Wind protection is one of the most important tasks of any gardener. One option is to erect some kind of barrier, either artificial or natural. In beginning to tackle wind problems, artificial barriers are really the only option, as sheltering hedges take a while to grow. In the long term it

pays to plant these wind blocks. Hedges and bushes protect the plants in their lee frodamage while still allowing for good air circulation.

Gardeners rarely feel that the ideal dose of rain has fallen just where it's needed. As vital as it is for plants to thrive, it is also problematic in excess. If you have well-drained soil, heavy showers or seemingly continuous rain will not cause too much havoc. Heavy soils should be conditioned with sand and organic matter. In some cases, the installation of a drainage system or even some kind of overhead protection for your plants is required. Too little rain can be remedied with a watering can or a built-in watering system. Up to a point, adding compost or a layer of mulch can also prevent dry soil to the soil.

We all need the sun, but each to very differing degree. Many woodland plants simply do not tolerate direct sunlight. Shade seekers should be planted underneath trees; otherwise you need to create an artificial sunshade for them. Less sun-sensitive plants will do very well with lots of sunshine as long as there is good, permanent moisture in the soil. If your plants develop leaf burn, it may be as a result of watering them in the heat of the sun. Drops of water can act as lenses, concentrating the sun's rays on the leaves of the plant and "burning" them. Watering at times of less intense sunlight or watering your plants only around their roots can prevent this.

Frost is not a bad thing, but if severe or persistent it will damage many plants. Initially the plant material above ground will die off, before the frost gradually penetrates below the ground—and the longer and more severe the frost, the deeper and harsher the effects. The cold may kill off the roots directly, or the soil may dry out from being frozen solid. The best frost protection for your garden is to steer clear of any frost-sensitive plants. However, if your preference for certain plants won't allow this, protection in the form of troughs or hedges is recommended. Another solution is to plant frost-tender varieties directly in front of a wall that will reflect the warmth of the sun.

JANUARY

ANNUAL PLANNING

This year everything will be better than last year – a popular New Year resolution for gardeners too. The best thing to do is to start work right away, as there is plenty to do, even in January. It's time to plan out your whole gardening year and select new plants. On a more prosaic note, it's also the time to cut back many shrubs and plants.

> Even the freezing cold does not condemn passionate gardeners to a life of inactivity. This is the perfect time of year to see which trees could do with a trim.

Herbaceous perennials have a place in any flower garden, as they have something to offer almost year round and will provide enjoyment for many years. Long winter evenings are an ideal time to make yourself familiar with these rewarding plants. You can decide which ones to plant where in March, how big the clusters of plants should be and how the new ones will go with existing perennials. A leisurely walk through your winter garden is the ideal time to mull over these options.

In winter the tops of most perennials die back in the cold, and in spring the rootstock is regenerated. This is why new ones should be planted at that time of year. There are also wild perennials, which don't place many demands on cultivated soil and are therefore ideal for woodland gardens.

Herbaceous ornamentals are a different matter, as they prefer a rich, well-drained and aerated soil. There are some sun-worshippers among them, as well as varieties that favour semi-shade or no direct sunlight at all. Some of these are very decorative perennials suitable for planting under trees, while others thrive well in open spaces. Yet another group is better suited to rockeries or water features. Perennials come in many different sizes, from 1.8 metres (6 ft) tall to lowly ground covers.

They also come in every imaginable colour, so you can group them according to height and colour tone. Low-growing border plants include aubretia "blue cushion", speedwell (veronica), stonecrop, moss phlox and alyssum. Mid-size perennials include oriental poppies, tickseed (coreopsis), daisies, salvias and irises, while monk's hood, some phlox varieties, delphiniums and foxtail lilies can grow to quite stately heights. All that remains is to check the flowering times so you will know which plants to choose to achieve the desired outcome.

Enough planning—let's head outdoors, where any weak undergrowth will have been trimmed back in December. Now you can use any frost-free days to make a start on the more vigorous undergrowth. This includes shrubs that bloom in summer, or after your lilac has flowered. You can delay pruning, but it is a good idea to make the most of the relative peace and quiet to remove any old wood on your ornamental shrubs. You will have

already noted the offending spurs in the previous year, i.e. those producing few flowers. Too many older branches drain the plant's resources and can lead to poor flowering, so removing some of these branches is a good idea. Be sure to apply this only to old shoots that are sapping the plant's energy, as flowering wood should not be trimmed or "knocked into shape" at this point. Shrubs that flower in spring should not be attacked with the secateurs either, as they will have already formed new buds.

Wild hedges are just as precious. They provide a valuable refuge for useful wildlife like hibernating hedgehogs and should not be disturbed. Any unnecessary wakening over the winter will sap their energy. You could also threaten the stability of birds' nests by thinning out hedges at this time of year, which would deprive you of a dawn chorus in spring and perhaps even dissuade birds from nesting in your garden at all.

Finally, take some time to glance around your vegetable garden. Brussels sprouts, leeks and kale should be able to hold their ground despite the cold, so on frost-free days you may still be able to pick some for dinner.

Fruit tree grafting is a task best completed in the first few months of the year.

If you attended to micro-habitats in autumn by providing over-wintering aids for beneficial creatures, you'll be delighted by a number of natural pest eradicators later on.

THE FIRST FLOWERS OF THE YEAR

Just as no real gardener is intimidated by frost and snow, there are plants that defy the cold and produce early flowers. Naturally they will generally choose the mildest days to pull one over the winter, but there are always a few brave ones that put in a surprise appearance – to the delight of all garden lovers.

The first snowdrops are always a welcome sign of the spring yet to come. With a little luck, the first daffodils will even be out by the end of January.

It's not yet the peak season for them, but when the icy wind pauses to draw breath and the winter sun paints circles of light on the bare branches of trees, they can sometimes be seen poking their noses out through the winter gloom. And should winter return with a vengeance, they may just defy the cold with the help of a little frost protection. Snowdrops can flower for weeks on end with this kind of assistance, as the cold keeps them fresh.

To make life a little easier for these early arrivals, you can choose a suitable site for their bulbs. Snowdrops prefer a moist soil, which is almost always guaranteed in the winter, and they will thank you by nodding their heads in approval if you place them along shrub borders or give them a little wind protection by planting them in front of a wall. They come out of the ground in clusters and their soil will need no extra attention once the bulbs have established

If these little white flowers think they will have the undivided attention of flower-hungry winter folk, they are quite mistaken. The very widespread winter jasmine, with its small, yellow, star-shaped blooms, also demands attention at this time of year. It doesn't have to try very hard, as its golden glow is very distinctive against the backdrop of white snow and bare branches, offering sunny respite in the dark days of winter. The winter jasmine thrives in rich, loamy soils and sunny, sheltered locations. It is a decorative way to enhance bare walls or slopes, as its branches trail nicely. For the same reason, it does require staking or securing to a wall or the side of the house. That way it will provide plenty of cheery colour at eye level to relieve the winter's gloom.

Another competitor for early line honours that doesn't just bloom in January (but is not afraid of the raw cold, either) is witch hazel. If you provide this often towering shrub—which can grow up to an impressive 4 metres (14 ft) high—with a sheltered spot, it will continue flowering right through from October. It tends to flower in winter as it originates from East Asia, where spring comes around in January.

Witch hazel (hamamelis) has particularly prominent flowers, as it throws off its leaves in the autumn and there is nothing to obscure its bushy, exotic, yellowish brown blooms. It acquired its name from two of its distinctive qualities: the leaves resemble those of the hazelnut, and its branch forks are popular for use as divining rods.

Three beautiful shrubs flowering at such an inhospitable time provide a lovely foretaste of spring. You can do even more to promote a spring feeling in the winter months by cultivating all kinds of plants in your greenhouse. It's not just a matter of creating colourful beauties for the eyes to feast on—now is the time to nurture a few spring vegetables and salad greens that will soon provide you with some vitamins that help shrug off any spring lethargy.

The few plants that flower in winter add a welcome splash of colour to the garden, especially in January. These include winter jasmine (above) and the Chinese witch hazel, also known as hamamelis (left).

BERRY CANES AND FRUIT TREES

We've already touched on the time for pruning flowering shrubs. Now it's the turn of berry canes, as they need to be encouraged to produce new shoots—but not if the temperatures drop below -5 °C (23 °F). It's important to realize that different berries need different pruning. It is also time to start grafting your stone and pip fruit scions.

For berries like currants or gooseberry bushes, January is a good time for rigorous pruning. Any weak spurs can be removed completely and vigorous ones just cut back a little, to encourage the plant to produce several new lead spurs that will bear fruit.

Redcurrants thrive best on two to three-year-old wood. If you haven't already pruned the canes right after harvesting your summer crop, now is the time to start. All spurs that are more than 5 years old (the darker wood) should be cut off at the base of the plant, leaving just two to three young spurs, and all other young shoots should be removed. The bush should not consist of more than eight to twelve shoots originating from the base of the plant. The bushes will reward you with a plentiful and good quality crop if you prune them well now.

The blackcurrant differs from its red cousin in that it thrives best on one-year-old spurs. For this reason, you should cut back the branches during your January pruning session right down to the young spurs in the lower third of the plant. Incidentally, it is much easier to do this right after picking the summer crop, as you can remove the upper branches—fruit and all—at the same time. If there are enough young spurs appearing from the root base, you can cut your blackcurrant bushes right back to ground level. Gooseberries, which primarily fruit on the previous year's laterals, can be treated like red-

young canes on the ground in late autumn and cover them with twigs.

If you would like to graft fruiting wood, the simplest way is to buy scions for grafting onto tree stock. However, you can also produce scions yourself by cutting suitable shoots or branches and storing them until grafting time in spring, when the danger of frost has passed.

In order to do this, select some of last year's branches that are about 30 cm (12 in) long and pencil-thick from strong, healthy fruit trees that produced tasty fruit. If they happen to come from the sunny side of the tree they will be particularly vigorous. Cut them off and label the top and bottom ends. Then plant a bundle of scions in soil in a shady, cool position. It is vital that they don't dry out or start growing, as they have to stay there till grafting time in March. The second half of January is the best time for cutting most fruit trees.

You can follow a similar approach with black-currants if you want to increase your crop. Cut off the spurs and store them the same way in a stack. To root them, simply place them in the soil in March.

Good hand tools for grafting are essential, including a splicing knife. (above).

Select only strong, healthy scions for grafting (left).

The success of grafting depends on scion and stock fitting together as closely as possible. If tied with raffia and treated with a suitable sealant, the graft should take (below).

currants, but raspberry canes require different pruning. You will have already trimmed the canes that cropped last season to just above ground level when you picked the last fruit. Any weak, unpromising looking new growth can also be removed until you have only eight to twelve canes per metre (yard) remaining. Prune these back a little more in January and you will end up with fewer but bigger berries. The same applies to grapevines, if you are interested in harvesting good quality grapes. Ideally you should only allow one spur to the right and one to the left of the main rod.

Blackberries on the other hand are better left unpruned at this time of year. They are very sensitive to the cold and will suffer serious damage at temperatures below -15 °C (5 °F). They will produce new shoots after they recover, but the whole crop will be a write-off. You can avoid the risk of this happening if you lay the

FRAMES AND HOT BEDS

Many of our bedding plants are annuals or biennials that only flower once and are then removed. They provide welcome variety alongside perennials and long-life shrubs. However, they have to be bought every year and planted out again. If you want to avoid doing this and prefer to reap what you have sown yourself, it's worth trying a cold frame.

Without using frames or greenhouses to protect our trays of seedlings, many cultivated plants wouldn't stand a chance of surviving the winter in some climates. Raising seeds or cuttings in trays or pots is the preferred method.

Cool frames and hot beds are terms used to describe different containers, frames and even entire greenhouses. They all serve the same purpose: they make it possible to use the inhospitable time of year to raise seedlings that would not stand a chance out in the open.

Sowing your own seeds has the advantage of giving you more choice, since ready-raised seedlings are nowhere near as prolific as the range of seeds available in retail outlets. You can raise seed in pots or trays, in containers or on flat, covered frames—with or without panels that open and shut automatically, and heated or unheated. A distinction is made between portable frames made of wood, aluminium or plastic (these are simply placed on the ground and can be moved around), and fixed or permanent containers made of concrete or bricks. You can use plastic film or glass to cover them and, depending on the temperature, open them on the side away from the wind using pegs or thermostatically controlled airing devices.

Hot beds are built in exactly the same way but tend to have electric heating or some method of adding warmth from biogas (which arises through the rotting of organic matter). Very practical, small, electric cultivation trays are available in some shops. Both cool and hot frames require high humidity and the type of soil that promotes sprouting (seed-raising mix). It must be kept moist by watering or by hanging a portable frame with a perforated floor in a container that allows it to absorb water up to half the depth of the soil layer.

Covering or cloching the frames works just like the panes of a greenhouse in trapping the

Vegetables that like warmth, such as capsicums or aubergines, are well off in a "cold frame". It doesn't have to be a deluxe version with automatically opening and closing vents—a wooden box covered with plastic sheeting is perfectly adequate.

Small greenhouses and cold frames are available in all shapes and sizes; sometimes they are even sold as kit sets.

heat, as the long-wave infrared rays are able to penetrate the pane or the plastic but are only partially reflected back outside again. Even in a so-called "cool frame"—one that uses only daylight—you can maintain relatively consistent temperatures that are well above the prevailing conditions outside the frame. If you don't have an automatic system, make sure that the containers are opened when the sun is shining or covered with mats to prevent undue heat from being trapped inside and damaging the plants.

Advice on what you should sow and when you can expect the seedlings to appear is included on the back of most seed packets. If you sow too early you run the risk of young plants maturing before its time to transplant them into the open. For smaller beds, seed rills are not necessary. Simply scatter the seed by hand as evenly as possible. Over coarser seeds pass a layer of seedling mix through a sieve. For fine seed (like begonia), it is sufficient to poke them in with a little water.

When the seedlings form their first pair of leaves, you should prick them out, transplanting them a little further apart from one another, in several different beds if necessary. When it is time to plant them outdoors, space them according to the recommendations on the seed packet.

PREPARATIONS FOR SUMMER

We have already talked about planning your herbaceous perennials for the warmer seasons, but there's a lot more to consider if you want to be rewarded with a rich tapestry of colour in the height of summer. Decisions now have to be made about your vegetable and flower garden, as this sort of preparation takes some time.

Let's begin with the ultimate ornamental: roses. They need care and attention at this time of year, as not all varieties survive the winter well. Some need protection. Unlike wild roses, most ornamental roses will not make it through the cold months without some assistance. The stems that still have a few leaves attached are most at risk but they are also the best to keep, if you can safely nurture them until the warmer months arrive. If you haven't already done so in late autumn, now is the time to protect your roses by banking up a good layer of soil and well-rotted manure about 20 cm (8 in) above the base of the plant. Protect the top of the plant with true fir branches, which are better suited to the purpose than white fir branches (boughs of white fir tend to dry out over time and drop their needles). This type of covering gives the roses a chance to gradually become used to more air and light. Sometimes

A little imagination is required to visualise a front garden like this in the middle of January, but now is the time to plan and plot your next moves. Will the summer flowers compliment the colour of the house? Which perennials go well with one another? What size crop do you want the vegetable garden to produce?

too much snow can accumulate on the protective cover, so keep checking to see whether it needs to be shaken off from time to time.

Many evergreens appreciate being watered on frost-free days. If the plants are young, they will need additional protection from the winter sun and the drying effect of the wind. Brushwood or straw provide beneficial cover and a layer of snow on top will be tolerated as long as it does not become too heavy. Young plants tend to be brittle, so shake off any excess snow with care.

Perhaps even more important than planning colour combinations, flowering sequences and the composition of your flower garden is the order in which your vege-

table crop should proceed. A basic principle to remember is that intensive cultivation of any one crop over time will take its toll on the soil. Gardeners and farmers have known this for centuries and have observed that each vegetable drains the soil of certain nutrients. Examples include:

Strong feeders: artichokes, cauliflowers, cucumbers, potatoes, drumhead cabbages, leeks, rhubarb, pumpkins, Brussels sprouts, celery and tomatoes

Moderate feeders: chicory, garlic, kohlrabi, swede, carrots, radishes, beetroot, salad greens, spinach, courgettes and onions

Weak feeders: most peas and beans or pulses.

For this reason, it is a good idea to divide your vegetable patch into three areas, so you can operate a miniature rotation system. The first year, plant the strong feeders in area one, the moderate feeders in area two and the weak feeders in area three. The following year, each type moves over one "field" until, in year four, you are back to the original layout. Of course compost should be added to each area every year.

One other thing to note for vegetable gardens is that not all plants like to share the same bed. Mixed cultures of "compatible" vegetables are recommended. Some highly compatible bedfellows are: salad greens, kohlrabi, radishes and peas; or carrots, lettuce and leeks; or tomatoes, parsley and garlic; or kale and dwarf beans.

Branches laden with snow can cause real problems, as younger trees in particular will not be able to cope, and may break under the strain (left).

A good layout and careful planning is particularly important if you want your patch to yield good fresh vegetables (below left).

It's a good idea to surround vegetable beds with low hedges, beams or wooden posts so you can access them easily and the soil always stays inside the plot (below).

FEBRUARY

THE FIRST GARDENING JOBS

February is definitely the month for early preparation, both inside and out. Cold frames not only provide an opportunity to overwinter any frost-sensitive ornamentals, but also help to harden open-air plants and cultivate any cuttings. On frost-free and dry days it pays to work the soil and lay out your garden plots.

February is a month of preparation, but also time to start working in the garden in earnest. You'll have your hands full in the vegetable garden but you also need to start propagating any annuals and seedlings.

Y ou will notice plenty of growth at this time of year—especially if you have cold frames. You need to prick out crowded seedlings and give them more room to grow. Be sure to keep seedlings from too much light to prevent them from maturing too early. It's time to propagate any annuals, as they are the ones that will provide renewed colour once the first spring bulbs such as tulips and daffodils are past their prime. Some varieties will light up the garden all summer long with their radiant colours. The following is a small selection: Beardlip penstemon, verbena, dianthus, monkey flowers, ageratum, stock, snapdragons, lobelia, Livingstone daisies, slipper flowers, petunias, red salvias, asters, purple cone flowers, butterfly flowers, ornamental tobacco plants and zinnias.

All these summer beauties are gentle on the soil and don't require much care from hobby gardeners, who often use them to complement other colour combinations. There are two groups to distinguish when cultivating annuals. Flowers that take a little longer to mature are best sown indoors from mid-February, under glass or in a heated greenhouse, and then transplanted a month later as seedlings. The faster maturing kinds can be sown directly outside in late spring.

Beds for vegetables and annual flowers can be prepared in February. Be sure to prepare beds promptly for any vegetables you'd like to set out early under a cold frame. The first outdoor jobs in the garden can be tackled on any frost-free, dry days. If you have finished planning the types of vegetables you are going to plant and where you'll put them, it is advisable to divide up your beds as follows: long beds to produce larger quantities of the same vegetable, and smaller plots if you want a little of each. Now is the time to mark out three areas for crop rotation and a fourth section for the plants that will always be grown in the same place, like strawberries or rhubarb. For mixed cultures you will need slightly bigger

beds than for a single variety. When designing the layout, bear in mind that vegetables thrive best if they are protected from the wind. Bushes on the windward side can be a useful form of protection, and hedges or tall sunflowers also serve as suitable wind blocks, keeping small wildlife and bees very happy at the same time. The distance between these protective plants should be carefully calculated to prevent them from shading your vegetables.

You can continue the work you began in late autumn on preparing the soil, weather permitting. Loosen up the clods with a garden fork to a good depth, without breaking up the soil structure too much, removing weeds as you go. Work in some well-rotted manure or organic compost and spread any raw compost on top. Any sections not worked over in autumn will have to be thoroughly dug now, after removing the top turf. The sods are the best form of compost and should be placed upside down on one of your compost heaps.

When creating new beds, dig down to at least the depth of two spades without mixing up the two layers of soil. The top soil is richer in nutrients, so make sure you leave it where the plants' roots can get at it, not dug way down at the bottom of the hole. You'll want to be just as careful if you have to go even deeper to ameliorate very hard ground.

When the ground slowly warms up in early spring and the worst frosts are over, you can begin conditioning the soil. A "wild sow tooth" (left), a specialized, sharp hoe from southern Germany, is good for breaking up clods. A garden fork will also do the job.

In cold frames (below) you can let the first plants grow to seedlings even in February's chill.

THE FIRST PLANTS OF THE YEAR

Spring is heralded by the first plants that pop up their heads despite a little snow that might remain on the ground. When early flowering plants such as crocuses, blue dwarf irises or buttercups start to emerge in the garden, it's time to sow some spinach in your vegetable patch.

Among the first plants that fight their way through even partially snow-covered ground are early crocuses like the 'Golden Bunch' variety. These robust and easy-care plants form large bunches over the years as they self-sow and proudly usher in the spring with their golden glow.

Perhaps the most famous crocus is a fall blooming one. Saffron not only turns cake a vibrant yellow, the plant *(crocus sativus)* also gladdens the heart when it breaks through the ground. No wonder ancient Egyptians and Romans were anxious to extract the pigment from the flower's style and dye their clothing in the rich golden hue. Saffron was prized almost as highly as purple. It took 100,000 crocus flowers to produce one kilogram of the pigment. Most of the nearly 80 varieties of crocus flower in March or April, but a few boldly poke up their heads in early February. Among them is the deep yellow variety "Golden Bunch" *(Crocus ancyrensis)* that seems to burst out through the dreary cold like a beacon of hope. This boldness is all the more surprising, given that the origins of this impetuous herald of spring lie in the Mediterranean and the Near East. Its beaming colour seems to capture some of the luminous light of the south.

More restrained, but nonetheless intense in colour, is the blue dwarf iris that won't allow the crocus to hog

the limelight. Its early appearance is a happy surprise, as the word "iris" most often makes us think of the German bearded iris, which arrives much later with the early summer palette of colours. The dwarf iris is one of over 200 iris varieties now available in the UK, many of which bear names more reminiscent of winter, such as "Alaska White" or "Siberian Iris".

A fully-grown dwarf iris stands no more than 20 cm (8 in) high. It can't afford to offer the biting wind too much of a target. Its summer counterparts in the warmer months can grow to just over 1 metre (3 ft), and some varieties that prefer the swampy ground near ponds can even reach as much as 50 cm (18 in) taller than that. Irises come in herbaceous perennial and bulb form. Most of them—apart from the swamp irises—enjoy a dry, well-drained, chalky soil.

Another plant of European origin that is not intimidated by winter is known as Yellow Pheasant's Eye. It bears the Latin name *Adonis vernalis*, because of its youthful beauty. Adonis was a model athlete of ancient Greece with whom Aphrodite, the patron of lovers and goddess of eroticism, fell in love. Sadly, the object of her desire was killed by a wild boar—probably with a little help from her jealous husband. The inconsolable Aphrodite is said to have made a flower grow from the blood of her loved one to serve as an eternal reminder of the beauty of Adonis. This pretty little flower

may seem a trifle insubstantial to carry the full weight of an ancient Greek tragedy. However, it has earned its right to bear the name, as it's bold nature has no fear of winter—though its enthusiasm does wane a little around the initial blossom period. Its yellow star-shaped blooms are an unmistakable sign of the new season. The lovely, but spreading, little wildflowers often called "Butter and Cream" are related to this plant. Cultivated varieties include 'Bowles Double' and 'Brazen Hussy,' which can emerge as early as February in sheltered conditions.

Apart from early flowering crocuses, 'Yellow Pheasant's Eye' (above) imbues the garden with the first flush of spring colour.

Spinach (left) can be sown outside from February onwards and is ready to pick in seven to eight weeks.

TYPES OF SOIL AND SOIL PREPARATION

Your success as a gardener depends to a very large degree on what you plant, where you sow, and in what type of soil. Not all soils are the same and the soil requirements vary from plant to plant. "Good" soil is therefore not an absolute term, but rather dependent on both the gardener's planting preferences and preparation skills.

Without soil, nothing will grow in your garden. The soil type (loamy, chalky or sandy, for example) is important, but so are the acidity and the lime content. Whether your soil is acid, neutral or alkaline substantially determines how your plants will grow, as they each have a natural preference for certain conditions.

An important factor in deciding what kind of earth to offer your plants is to check whether the unprepared ground in your garden plot is basically alkaline (limey) or acidic (lime-free) in nature. Certain plants have a definite preference for one type of soil or the other. Rhododendrons, for instance, will form stronger roots in acidic soil, while other garden plants—most others, in fact—prefer neutral soil, that is, soil that is neither particularly alkaline nor particularly acidic.

It's not complicated to run a soil check, and it should be done before you begin preparing the ground for the first planting. Soil tests are based on chemicals that react to the level of pH (a Latin term, *potentia hydrogenii*, meaning "hydrogen concentration") in your soil. The pH value of water is considered to be neutral at 7. Lower values move in an acidic direction on the scale, while higher numbers denote an alkaline tendency. Vegetables, fruit trees, plus many perennials and shrubs like a slightly acidic soil, preferring a pH rating between 6.5 and 7. Ratings below 5.5 will cause problems for them and also allow too many undesirable weeds to thrive. High alkaline readings greater than 8 point to a lack of nutrients (iron, magnesium, etc). That can lead to stunted growth and little to no harvest, though an iron deficiency is easily recognisable on fruit trees or roses by their yellowing foliage. However, soil deficiencies can only be augmented to a certain degree by artificial means.

It is definitely better to concentrate on plants that can cope well with an alkaline soil, such as roses, all kinds of brassica, wallflowers, carna-

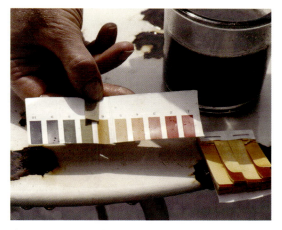

tions, beeches, box hedges and clematis—to name but a few. They are much less likely to suffer for being planted in chalky soil. Some plants will tolerate both kinds of soil but react differently in each case. Typical hydrangeas, for instance, will flower blue in acidic soil and pink in limey soils, while in neutral ground they produce more purple-blue blooms.

To lower the pH level of a soil, or to prevent excessive build-up of lime, you can introduce large quantities of leaf litter and well-rotted compost—digging it in every year. If you want to increase the amount of lime in an acidic soil, simply add garden lime. It's best to do this in winter after turning the clods. Simply leave the lime on the

surface and do not add any manure that year. Lime additions improve the ground structure of heavy soils and lighten their texture. If you have sandy soil, you will have to add lime more often, as it will be washed away by rainfall. You should also lightly work in any clay or silicate rock powder during the winter. If you have highly acidic soil, don't try to improve it all at once. Instead, it is preferable to add about 500 gr (1 lb) of lime per square metre (10 square ft) each winter for several years in a row.

Different layers of soil are easy to identify on exposed slopes (above).

You don't really need a chemical lab to determine the acid content of your soil. With the help of simple soil test kits you can carry out your own analysis (centre).

A proliferation of rain worms is a sure sign of a soil rich in nutrients and humus (below).

PROPAGATING

Many plants benefit from being raised under cover before they venture into the open. If you don't have a greenhouse you can raise seedlings in a living room kept at a constant temperature, a conservatory or even on a windowsill. The crucial thing is not to overheat them, as the occasional cold spell to toughen them up will do no harm.

You don't need any particular equipment in order to raise plants from seed. Seedlings can be raised indoors in a normal wooden box or in peat pots while there's still a blanket of snow on the ground outside.

Propagation works well in peat pots, boxes or crates, depending on the quantities you want to raise. Flowering bulbs are particularly suited to indoor pots. They are some of the most beautiful ornamental flowers of any spring garden and can be combined well with other plants. A distinction is made between bulbs, rhizomes and tubers, but many people refer to all of them as bulbs or tubers without making a finer distinction.

the bulb, as in the daffodil, tulip and onion (hence its visible layers). Tubers, on the other hand, are either root sections that have thickened to form a storage base—such as the potato—or swollen underground stems, such as lily of the valley, which is strictly speaking a rhizome. For simplicity's sake, we will refer to them all as bulbs.

Flowering bulbs are ideal candidates for growing wild. They can be spread about in lawns and wooden tubs and help to create a natural setting. Bulbs you have raised this month to the point of just before full bloom can be planted out the following month. If you would prefer not to wait and would rather enjoy a touch of spring indoors, you can even raise bulbs in autumn. Then you will have daffodils and crocuses flowering in February in all different colours along your windowsills. However, bulbs raised in this way won't be suitable for planting out. You will have to wait until after summer when they have finished flowering to put them in the ground.

A bulb is a modified shoot with layers of fleshy scales that store reserved plant food. In some bulbs, the swollen scales completely envelop

Raising your own seedlings is a good way of getting exactly what you want. Old or not strictly labelled seed you have collected yourself might prove unsuitable. For this reason, it is worthwhile running a germination test. Put some moist sand or a thin layer of light soil into a flat tray and plant a few seeds wrapped up in wet blotting paper or simply added as they are. Cover the tray with plastic wrap or a glass lid and leave in a well-heated room (around 21 °C/70 °F).

Depending on the type of plant, germination will happen very quickly (in the case of hollyhocks or beans around ten days), or take quite a while—snapdragons, for instance, take over three weeks. You can tell how many seeds are actually germinating much earlier if you check the base of the blotting paper with a magnifying glass. If you get a 75 percent success rate, you have excellent seeds. The lower the strike rate, the closer together you should sow the seed. If less than a quarter of the seed germinates, it is not worth continuing to use that batch.

When cultivating from seed, bear in mind that light-germinating seed must not be covered, while dark-germinating seed requires it. Sage, carrots, lettuce or campanula need light, so the seed can just be scattered over the soil in a box and kept in a light place. Delphiniums, petunias or pansies will only germinate in the dark. They should be covered with a thin layer of earth; 5 mm (¼ in) is usually sufficient. For direct sowing in the open later on, you will need to mark out a seed row or "drill" and then cover it with earth.

If you want a foretaste of spring indoors, plant some early bulbs in pots. To make sure you get the timing right, you will need to lift the bulbs or tubers out of the ground the autumn before you would like them to bloom.

PLASTIC SHEETING AND FLEECE

Even if the end of winter is nigh, the amount of sunshine you are likely to get in February is limited. This doesn't mean plants in seed beds that are too big to keep indoors will have to freeze, as modern technology has come to the rescue with a wide range of protective plastic sheeting and fleece.

> Premature maturity and frost protection are the main reasons why protective covers are used in the garden. Particularly in a vegetable garden, you can achieve great success with a variety of different covers.

Plastic is indeed fantastic, and plastic manufacturers certainly have developed some ingenious products these days, like wafer-thin, flexible and even breathable plastics and polythenes. These transparent or light-reflecting covers are useful at this time of year, as frost can still be expected some days, or rather nights—and those cold spells put germinating or recently sprouted seeds at risk.

These covers have to be thin so that they don't weigh down the young plants, but they also have to keep the heat in. Paradoxically, the fact is that the thinner they are, the warmer they keep the plants. The sheets of plastic don't lie directly on the plants, but instead trap a layer of air between the cold ground and themselves, which is then warmed according to the same principle as a greenhouse. The heat of the light—no actual sunshine is required—penetrates through the clear film and is trapped inside; only a small amount is released again. Even at freezing temperatures your covered beds will stay in the frost-free. Pimpled plastic sheeting is especially effective.

These covers, whether clear or opaque, also help guard against another classic threat. Sometimes it's not snow that does the damage, but dry cold, as the ground in which seedlings are germinating can become quite parched. Plastic sheeting stops moisture from evaporating—as is evident in the condensation that form on its inside surface. Since there are a whole range of frost-germinating plants, which actually require the cold to

begin growing, opaque films that trap less heat are also suitable.

Some plastic covers are also called mulch covers. If you use black ones, they will have a heating effect, as they absorb the light and don't reflect it. For frost-germinating plants these are not as suitable at this time of year, though they do have the advantage of helping other plant types that will benefit from the warmth. Unlike the transparent options, they will also prevent unwanted weeds from appearing, while at the same time keeping the ground nice and moist. The stronger the sun, the greater the heat generated, of course. Once the plants appear above ground and push against the mulch cover, you can cut slits and holes in the surface to let them through, while the weeds remain trapped underneath. You can also pop plants straight through the holes to plant them, but that is not a job for this time of year. Cutting holes is not necessary in the case of transparent sheeting with pre-cut slits, which come in very handy next month (see overleaf), when more intense growth occurs. These sheets actually expand with the plants, as the slits stretch and even let rainwater through.

The same permeability is also a feature of horticultural fleeces, which are made out of woven man-made fibres. They are constructed much like a piece of gauze, and keep plenty of pests at bay. You can also get porous plastic sheeting meant specially for plants that grow on wires or stakes. They are placed over the plants like plastic bags but allow for air circulation. Other, curved arrangements allow you to build proper tunnels that offer germinating plants plenty of room to grow to a certain height.

As you can see, with all these materials and different options, it pays to think hard about the right kind of cover to suit your particular purposes before you make a purchase.

To ensure that covers do not fly away in a gust of wind, anchor them to the ground with hooks or stones (above left).

Plastic sheeting is normally used in flat beds but can also cover staked tomatoes (above right).

Mulch covers, mainly black ones, prevent the soil from drying out and also stop weeds from seeing the light of day (below left).

Plastic covers used for tunnels are robust yet very light (below right).

MARCH

THE END OF THE WINTER SEASON

Now it's time to remove all protective layers from your frost-tender plants, air the lawns, prepare vegetable plots, plant ornamental and fruit trees, prune ornamental shrubs, sow seeds and plant seedlings. What you fail to do this month will haunt you the rest of the year, and what you achieve in March will pay off right through until autumn.

Any leaves, pine needles or straw that have been protecting your more sensitive plants throughout the winter may, and in fact must, now disappear from your garden beds. If you leave them on too long they will inhibit the growth of your plants. And conditioning the soil is definitely the order of the day. As little is done in the garden over the winter, water and frost can have a hardening effect on the topsoil. Bulbs like tulips and crocuses will then find it hard—sometimes too hard—to reach their full potential. A handheld hoe or garden fork will allow you to loosen up any hard soil, without hurting your plants.

As for sowing seeds, apart from the conventional seed packets or seed strips, you can now buy some seeds in pill capsule form. These are high quality products that you can rely on to produce a healthy plant every time. Put two or three capsules in a pot or a small hole in the garden, where the shell will simply decompose and the seed will germinate. An exact dose of fertiliser within the pill capsule ensures rapid and healthy growth.

Planting seeds outside in March is not without some risk, due to the unpredictable night frosts that can sometimes occur. This is why a cold frame is a good idea as a form of protection at this time of year (see also page 24). This consists of a box-shaped wooden frame set on a wooden or concrete base and covered with glass or plastic sheeting. The frame over the base is set at an angle so rainwater can run off. A roll-up mat made of reeds will allow you to regulate the amount of sunshine the plants receive, but don't cosset them too much. Hardening them off will better prepare them for transplanting later on. When the weather is relatively good, air the frame by lifting it up to the height of a clod on the side facing away from the wind. Some garden shops sell ready-made frames with plastic lids. After a good month, the seedlings will be strong enough to take the next step into the open.

Pay some attention to trees and shrubs in March, as well. Any autumn leaves still lying around can be raked together and composted or worked into the soil at the base of your plants. Organic fertiliser can also be dug into the loosened soil at this stage.

Summer and autumn flowering ornamentals should be pruned in March, while spring flowering ones are best left until the bloom period is over. Summer flowering plants should be thinned out at this point. This includes perennial shrubs, which can be cut right back

At the beginning of the vegetation period, bulbs and tubers will appreciate having the soil around them loosened gently with a garden fork.

to ground level in March: bluebeard, bush clover, the Himalayan indigo bush (prune to about 30 cm/12 in above ground) and California lilac (ceanothus). However, there are some ornamental shrubs that don't appreciate any pruning at all: "Golden Rain" laburnum, magnolias or witch hazel should be left unpruned.

Azaleas are rhododendrons but, unlike the larger evergreen shrubs, they lose their leaves—with the exception of the magnificent Japanese azaleas. Both need similar treatment and appreciate acid soils, semi-shade and high humidity. That is why it is vital to water them very early in the year. You can improve the flower crop by enhancing them with special rhododendron fertiliser that you lightly work into the ground, but be careful when digging, as rhododendrons are shallow rooting. They don't need regular pruning, but if they start taking over, March is the right time to trim them back. Old bare branches can be cut back to 1 metre (3 ft) above ground level and new shoots will appear on the ends of the trunk.

Have a quick glance at the lawns too. At this time of year they will look quite tatty, even if you have been keeping them well raked. If you

want them to act as a soft green carpet in the summer, now is the time for plenty of TLC. Remove moss, dead grass and leaf mulch by raking or scarifying the surface, top dress the lawn—ideally with so-called controlled release fertiliser that will last until the autumn—and then water with a sprinkler.

In March some kinds of vegetables can be directly planted out. The normal method is to sow seed in marked rows.

Ornamental shrubs like the bottlebrush buckeye can be propagated by dividing the root growth. Spring is a good time of year to do this as root formation is at its most prolific and any divisions will come away quickly.

Heralds of spring, such as the silver catkins of the pussy willow shown here, ring in a new cycle of growth. The gloom of winter will soon be gone.

EARLY BLOOMERS

Gardeners can enjoy plenty of early blooms before the onset of true spring, from daphne to pussy willow and from yellow jasmine to crocuses. Keen perennial growers will be in their element and have their hands full ensuring that a fresh supply of new flowers follow after the first flush of spring.

If you pruned your perennials well back in late autumn (i.e., back to about 15 cm [6 in] above ground), your plants will now be ready for their spring makeover. Protective stubble that has formed over the cold winter months will need to be removed right down to ground level, as the plant will survive well without it when new shoots grow.

You can encourage their growth by loosening up the soil at the base of your plants, taking out any weeds and "feeding" each plant as soon as it begins to sprout. The best idea is to spread compost or bone meal around the plant. Work it into the soil and leave some compost lying on top. Use your gut instinct to decide the right quantity, as there really is no such thing as too much or too little. "Feeding" plants must also include thorough watering.

In the preceding months you will have prepared the soil for any new perennials, and this is the time to begin planting them. Choose a day when the sun is not shining directly to add organic compost to the prepared plots, working it in and smoothing it over afterwards. The next step is to divide the flowerbed into sections for the individual plants.

You should design the layout with taller plants at the back and shorter ones in front, as this will give the garden a nice tiered look. The effect will also be improved if you plant groups of three to five of one variety together. Leave plenty of room between the groups so you don't have to divide up the roots again after the first season of growth. The initial gaps between plants can be filled with annuals if you wish. This also promotes growth, as plants, like people, generally prefer company.

Here's how to plant: most perennials are sold in containers. Check to see that the root bale is moist enough. As this is quite often not the case, it is recommended to water the plants beforehand, so they get a good drink before the upheaval of planting. Place them in the ground as deep as they were potted in their original containers.

Press the earth firmly around newly planted perennials and give them plenty of water in the weeks following planting. This promotes root growth. New plants are almost always thirsty, as they want to grow rapidly. There are, by the way, a range of perennials that are not suitable

for planting in spring. These include peony roses (best time: August/September), irises (June to August) and bleeding heart *(dicentra)*, which is best planted in autumn.

For lovers of native wild perennials, a word of advice here. They provide a valuable life support system for local wildlife and help keep the natural habitat in harmony. But there is no need to go out under cover of darkness to "snaffle" them from your local woods or, heaven forbid, nature reserves. Removing wild plants can damage natural areas, and in many places is prohibited by law. You will find all the plants you need in garden centres. This has the added advantage of ensuring the plants are designed to flourish in cultivated gardens. Such specimens will give you pleasure for longer than any ill-gotten gains.

The shady spots around your house and garden are also suitable for some perennials. Ferns are recommended in these areas, as they are rather uncomplicated wild plants. They enjoy the cooler temperatures and thrive perfectly well in quite shady areas underneath trees and between shrubs. March is the ideal time for them, as they prefer a rich humus soil. Spread some leaf litter down where you want them to grow. These ancient fan-shaped plants provide a good backdrop or scene setter for other plants. Depending on their location and purpose, you can choose between tall ferns (up to a metre/3 ft), medium height (about 45 cm/ 18 in when fully grown) or low-growing varieties that do not reach more than two or three hand-widths in height. Ferns will thank you for a layer of bark mulch or wood chips subsequent to being planted.

Ferneries do not necessarily have to be without colour, either, as some adjoining perennials will be particularly well set off by a backdrop of deep green ferns, such as foxgloves and astilbes, bugbane and anemones. Rhododendrons in full bloom also look stunning with a fringe or foreground of ferns nestling in their shade. When the flowering season is over, you end up with a wonderful array of different green tones ranging from pale lime to dark forest.

March is the month when the sun slowly but surely begins gathering some strength. In some regions, hazelnut catkins begin coming out at this time of year.

The blossoms of the coltsfoot, tussilago farfara, (above left) and the winter aconite (below left) are another unmistakable sign that the time for doing nothing in the garden is over.

SOWING SEEDS IN YOUR VEGETABLE GARDEN

March is the right time to sow if you want a good crop early in the season. It's also the month for raising seedlings in trays and cold frames, as well as taking appropriate steps to ensure seedlings are protected and develop quickly to full maturity. Different plants prefer plastic sheeting or fleece but there are some ground rules common to all plants.

Peat pots are an ideal method for germinating new seeds, as the container and the substrate are one and the same thing. It is important to keep pots made out of pressed peat well watered, as they dry out easily, causing the sensitive seedlings to wilt.

As some of what you need to know about seeds is written on the back of seed packets, we won't go into too much detail here, but whatever you do, make sure you loosen up the soil before sowing any seeds. Sowing vegetables in rows has proved its worth over the years and every garden centre sells suitable tools for marking out rows and drills. These allow you to sow seed of different sizes quickly and evenly.

Never place the seed too deep in the soil as the seedling may suffocate. You will find the correct depth shown on the packet. After covering the seed with earth, water the spot well and keep the

soil nice and moist until the first shoots are visible. It's worthwhile marking each row with plant sticks—at both ends, ideally—and in the middle too if you have very long rows. Another handy tip is to plant faster growing radishes between rows of carrot to indicate where the carrots might be.

There are a wide variety of methods available for speeding up the growing process. Hot beds are all the rage, as these create a warm climate in which seeds can germinate. There has to be the right balance of warmth and humidity for this to work.

The simplest method is to use plastic sheeting. It should not be a rigid plastic, but something flexible that will grow with the seedlings, like slit film with openings that will expand. These are placed loosely over the seeds and fastened at the side with stones or tucked under a frame. Insects and bad weather will not be able to do much damage to the seedlings unless there is a severe frost.

Plastic sheeting does not need to be ventilated and can stay in place for various lengths of time.

In the case of radishes, spinach and lamb's lettuce, for example, it can remain until the crop is ready, but lettuce will improve in flavour if left uncovered about two weeks before it is ready to pick. Kohlrabi, cauliflower, leeks and kale should only be left under plastic for six to ten weeks. Vegetables like cucumber, beans or strawberries will only tolerate plastic film until they flower, as they must be pollinated to produce a crop. It's advisable not to remove the cover in direct sunlight as this sudden exposure may put the plants into shock.

Other options include acrylic fleece, which lasts longer but does not grow with the plants and therefore has to be replaced at frequent intervals, or plastic tunnels on wire frames that can be purchased ready-made. The ones with ventilation holes are best. Garden outlets even sell complete cold frames in all shapes and sizes.

They can be permanently fastened or kept mobile so you can adjust the setting to the changing wind and sun direction. Once the seedlings sprout, shade should be provided in the form of straw matting to protect the young plants from night frosts. The seedlings need to be gradually introduced to the outside air (for more on films, fleeces and frames, see page 38). In milder, southern parts of the country, some vegetables may be planted out this month, but in the north it pays to wait a little longer. Vegetables suitable for sowing at this time of year are watercress, swede, carrots, lettuces, radishes, beetroot and spinach.

Other young plants or bulbs will not object to being put outside at the beginning of spring—if necessary with the addition of protective plastic. These include onions, shallots and garlic, early forms of lettuce and kohlrabi (turnip).

Planting aubergines outdoors is too risky in March, but you can start growing them under glass without any problems.

PRUNING FRUIT TREES

Fruit tree owners now need to swing into action. As the main focus is not on the short flowering season but rather on the final crop, it's best not to let young trees sprout away to their heart's content. Proper pruning at this point will ensure they stay in good shape and also bear plenty of tasty fruit at harvest time.

Once you plant any new fruit trees, your pruning shears will become one of your most hard-working tools. Newly planted apple or pear trees must be given a formative cut, like any other fruit tree, to ensure the desired growth occurs. Pruning also accelerates the budding process.

First identify the main shoot and remove any competing stalks or branches, i.e. any shoots that point upwards like the main leader. They need to be cut right back to the trunk of the tree. Then it's a matter of establishing which ones are the leaders—about three or four other major shoots. They will later form the top of the tree, so they need to grow at different heights along the trunk. You also need to make sure you have good symmetry right around the tree. If several branches seem suitable, the most horizontal ones should be the first choice, as they will bear more fruit. All the others should be cut off at the base of the tree. Only shorten the smaller shoots by about a third.

Every subsequent pruning in March over the next five years or so is called training or maintenance pruning, but it follows similar rules to the first formative cut. This time of year is ideal for pruning sensitive trees like peaches, as they come from the Mediterranean and will not tolerate earlier trimming in February. The canopy of the tree, especially in the case of the peach, must be kept small for it to thrive and for the gardener to be rewarded with plenty of fruit. Peaches and other fruit trees should be pruned annually in the following way:

Shorten the main spur and remove any competing shoots

Cut off any competing shoots on the leaders

Cut back all shoots of an upright nature

Remove all growth from the inside of the framework and any dead shoots.

The rationale behind this advice is that upright shoots grow rapidly but do not contribute anything to cropping. The main spur is particularly fast growing and needs to be cut back every spring. The actual fruiting wood will develop from the horizontal shoots. The same is also true of the laterals on main branches.

You can tell whether a fruit tree has been well looked after if it develops strong upward shoots. If it does, you will need to take the shears to it even more radically the next time around. If the opposite is true, naturally, the reverse applies: cut it back less.

After you have pruned your fruit trees, the question arises, as it does every year: where will

It's best to prune blackberries in spring before they begin to bud. Attach the stalks to a wire frame and train them in an arch shape in both directions.

I put this enormous pile of shoots and branches? Many local governing bodies now prohibit the burning off of garden waste, and neighbours seldom appreciate big clouds of smoke. Some local authorities provide a pick-up service for garden waste and it may even be free of charge. However, shredding or chipping is becoming increasingly popular. Please make sure that the noise level stays within permissible limits, as it is a very loud process. Some quieter models are now available. Shredders are not particularly expensive and very robust, but if you don't want to invest in one yourself, you can always hire one for the day. This will allow you to use a powerful model you could not afford to buy

yourself—especially if you have particularly thick branches to deal with. The end product also makes excellent mulch for your garden.

Finally, take a look around your orchard, as it won't look good unless the surroundings are also well maintained. Paths are a particularly important part of the process. There is nothing nicer than an evening stroll under blossom covered trees or branches laden with fruit. Inviting paths are what you want. Though moss creeping up between the stones or cracks may look quite pleasant, weeds and grass are generally less attractive.

As tiring as it is, removing unwanted growth from your paths is always better done with a garden knife than with any chemical substances. However, if you don't have the endurance to manually weed paths on a regular basis, garden outlets now stock relatively harmless products for eradicating weeds. Follow the instructions on the pack very carefully to ensure other plants or your own body are not damaged in the process. As paths are often arranged to allow rainwater to drain off the sides, you should hold off applying any chemical products until a fine day arrives. Otherwise your lawn along the edge of the path could suffer the consequences.

The so-called open or cup-shaped canopy is good for sour cherries, peaches and plums. Unlike the pyramid shape, these trees have no central spur. The tree will not bear as big a crop, but the quality of the fruit will be better.

Apple trees can develop a massive canopy over the years. Unpruned and left to their own devices, such trees are a joy to behold. However, the crop will reduce in size as the tree ages.

ROSE BEDS

The queen of all flowers needs the tender loving care of the gardener early in the year, as its true beauty depends on it receiving the right treatment. This is true not only of the rose bush itself but also of the surrounding area where it blooms—whether it be framed by lavender, a dark clump of junipers or a bed of competing lilies.

Spring cleaning in the rose beds should only be carried out on a dull day so the plants are not subjected to sunstroke after a long winter's night. Beneath their protective covers, the delicate young shoots and buds will not have had time to store enough of the natural pigment that protects them from the sun, anthozyan. But it is now high time to remove any remaining protective twigs, even from tall standard roses. If they have become bent over or covered in soil, they will need to be released gently and "unpacked". Leave tall standard roses in their bent position for a couple of days before carefully unwinding them and attaching them to their stakes.

At the end of March it is time to fertilise the ground and remove any mounds of soil. Loosen up the ground around the base of the plants and work in an organic, all-purpose compost or special rose fertiliser. Any piled up organic matter from the winter can be spread out on the ground and lightly worked into the soil as well. Then give the roses a good drink with plenty of water.

Planting roses in spring? Normally you see rose lovers out in autumn eagerly planting their new specimens. However, in some exposed areas there is too much heavy, wet soil and a great risk of frost kill. This is why

As a general rule, bush roses only need to be cut back when their blossoming vigour seems to be diminishing.

the spring is often preferred for planting roses, although a smaller crop of blooms is to be expected in the first year. Frost damage is a much worse prospect. Roses in containers, as they are often sold these days, may be planted right through the summer.

Without the right growing environment, however, even the healthiest roses will not survive. Well-drained, deep-seated, loose soil and an airy, sunny position are essential. Before planting, bare-root rose bushes should be left standing for about twelve hours in water. Then remove any broken roots and shorten the others a little, as this will stimulate particularly vigorous root growth. When you do any formative pruning, leave four to five eyes on each stem for floribundas or hybrid teas and cut away any broken or bruised shoots. Double the number of eyes should be retained on bush and climbing roses. Make sure you dig a deep enough hole for the plant—at least 60 cm (2 ft)—as the earth underneath the rose has to be nice and light too. The plant itself does not require this much depth, as it is sufficient to have the graft at about 5 cm (2 in) below ground level. The rest of the hole should be filled in. Enrich the soil with compost and make sure the roots are spread evenly around the hole. Firmly tread the soil without stamping too hard, and give it a good watering afterwards to ensure close contact is made between roots and soil. In the case of climbing roses, place the plant at a slight angle to the climbing frame. Before planting any long-stemmed, standard roses, ram a supporting stake into the ground first.

Five Golden Rules of Pruning

Each rose has its own pruning requirements. But the follow ground rules apply:

1) Broken or damaged shoots should be the first to be removed, down to the good wood.

2) The more you cut a shoot back, the stronger and longer it will grow.

3) As fatter spurs develop more (and stronger) shoots than thinner ones, cut the fat ones back slightly less than the thin ones.

4) If you want to achieve long-stemmed blooms on hybrid teas, you will need to prune the plants quite heavily. For shorter blooms, cut a little less off.

5) Always prune 1 to 2 cm ($^1/_2$–$^3/_4$ in) above buds that are growing away from the plant's centre (eyes), so that the new shoot will grow outwards and thrive.

Yes, it is definitely spring now, but it is still advisable in some areas to keep freshly planted rose shoots covered with a layer of protective mulch or organic cover. This should be at least 20 cm (8 in) high. It helps the plant to withstand the unpredictable weather conditions often experienced in March. About four weeks after planting, the protective cover can be removed.

The best time for pruning is early spring.

After planting your roses, tread the soil firmly and give them plenty of water.

APRIL

APRIL WEATHER

The fourth month of the year is renowned for being fickle: it either pours with rain or is almost as sunny as in summer. Though most of us moan about the showers, we tend to forget how beneficial such "bad weather" is for the garden. It saves us from constant watering and provides plenty of moisture—which is just what young plants and seedlings need at this time of year.

> April provides ideal growing conditions for new plants. If you propagate pampas grass, for instance, by dividing it in the spring, it will reward you with a silvery white show in September and October.

While we are on the subject of rain, all plants prefer rainwater to tap water—and it's free, so collecting rainwater is well worth doing. There are drums or barrels on the market suitable for collecting water from your guttering. You can shorten the down pipe and attach a bend at the height of the barrel, but this can lead to problems when the barrel overflows. A more elegant solution is to attach a piece of pipe with a valve outlet. This can be closed when the container is full. The barrel should definitely have a lid to keep out undesirable materials. Dirt will not do the plants any harm, of course, but other undesirable things like mosquito larvae can make the barrel their home, as they love any open water. If the lid is too loose, place a brick or stone on top to weigh it down.

Your garden needs large quantities of water at this time of year, as you will be sowing, pricking out and planting, and you need to water after each step. Even new pots need watering, regardless of whether they are made of terracotta or peat. All pots should be soaked in water before use by placing them in a deep basin. Pots made of pressed peat need more careful treatment as they may even disintegrate when totally saturated.

However lovely the scenery, garden paths will often be very wet this time of year and in some cases in poor shape after the winter. As you now have some time to spare between all the spring gardening jobs, check to see whether any of your paths need repairing or even relaying. Your plants will not have had time to spill over the edges yet, so you will be able to tidy up the full width of your paths. It's a good idea to think about making all plants easily accessible from one firm path.

Gravel is an effective way to combat wet walkways, as is a new coating of bark chips. These can be trodden into the path to create a firm surface. Once you have worked in all the dry material, water it with the garden hose to ensure a better bond is formed between the mulch and the soil.

Now is also the time to think about all the little things you will need to keep within an arm's reach. Hardwearing garden aprons are often forgotten, but these are very handy, unless you want to wash all your clothes after each little job you do in the garden. Aprons with large pockets are ideal for holding all the bits and pieces you need on the job. Secateurs and knife, pencil and string should all find room in your mobile garden shed.

String or raffia is good for keeping seed rows straight, plus sticks and string are ideal for keeping track of your delicate little carrots and radishes. If these fail to sprout or wilt quickly, or the lawn doesn't grow as you'd hoped, you may have an annoying problem on your hands. It's possible that some kind of larva has attached itself to the roots. These hungry little pests tend to hunt in packs in most gardens, so you can usually identify what kind of insect you are dealing with quickly. Act immediately by using a suitable pest control method. These days some very good organic products are available, so you don't necessarily have to use poisons to stay on top of them.

No vegetable garden is complete without kitchen herbs. Parsley, chives or dill should be sown outdoors anytime from April onwards so you will have a plentiful supply of fresh herbs in the summer.

Leafy vegetables are best sown from April onwards. Make sure when planning your rows that you have easy access to all the beds.

TULIPS, DAFFODILS AND LILIES

These flowers are a welcome sign that the days are getting warmer. Good combinations of all three will produce a pleasant mix of fragrance and colour. The composition of a bed for tulips, daffodils and lilies can be quite engaging, as the special qualities of each one must carefully be brought into balance with the others.

There are two planting times for bulbs and tubers. The more important one is in autumn, when all spring and summer flowering bulbs are on sale. Spring, on the other hand, is the time to choose summer and autumn flowering varieties, such as the Turks cap lily.

The main source of colour this month comes from many different varieties of flowers that will continue to bring pleasure over several weeks. Early tulips, including wild or waterlily tulips, generally show themselves at the beginning of the month. They are normally low-growing plants that can be dotted around the garden at will. Most varieties bloom at Easter time, generating beautiful tapestries of many different colours. Late tulips continue flowering until well into the merry month of May and the fullness of the double varieties makes them resemble peony roses.

Tulips show to best advantage when planted in groups. They provide a nice touch of colour to your lawn, but every three years their location should be changed so that the goblet-shaped blooms retain their brilliance. Any that come up "twisted" or malformed may be suffering from mould. In that case you have no choice but to remove the bulbs and destroy them. They are no good in your compost, as they could "infect" it and render it useless on your garden.

Daffodils display only a few sunny shades. They tend to be limited to pink, white and orange to yellow. They also make a colourful show for several weeks and are even better suited to naturalizing than tulips. There is no need to move them around, either. They form beautiful islands of colour that not even field mice will disturb.

However, sometimes daffodils do not grow the way you want them to. If the foliage turns yellow and dies off, it is a sure sign that the root action has stopped. Bulb fly may be the culprit in such cases. The only thing to do if this occurs is to lift the bulbs out and soak them in water for two days. The flies don't like this and will soon get the message that they are not welcome. The procedure can be shortened by immersing the bulbs in hot water of about 43/44 °C (110 °F) for two hours. This will kill the pests without hurting the bulbs. They won't flower again that year, but will recover and bloom again the following year.

A word of advice: daffodils are very hardy cut flowers, but they do not appreciate company. The milky liquid they produce will poison any other cut flowers, so always place them in a vase of their own. They add a lovely touch of spring to any room.

The third member of the April trio is the lily, which comes in a vast array of different forms from the turkscap to the trumpet variety. These long-lasting, hardy bulbs vary greatly in colour and size. We often plant them in autumn, but you can also plant them now to avoid the risk of any not surviving a particularly harsh winter.

Many gardening enthusiasts believe lilies are hard to grow, but this is a fallacy. Once plants get this kind of reputation, it is hard to shake it off, as gardening is very much passed on by word of mouth. This is definitely a case of bad press. You only have to look at all the farmers' gardens, where you see great clumps of lilies that have not been given much attention at all. Once these plants have found the right growing conditions, they are so easy to look after they can largely be left to their own devices.

Choose a sunny, wind-free and warm position for your lilies. Make sure you provide the moist, cool (not wet!) soil that lilies love, even after they take root—and keep watering them regularly. You can help them out by planting some decorative undergrowth around them or spreading some mulch at their feet.

Loosen humus-rich soil to a good depth before planting any lilies, then make a hole that is approximately 24 cm (10 in) deep. A good rule of thumb is to make the hole three times as deep as the bulb is high. Put a drainage layer of coarse sand about 5 cm (2 in) thick on the base of the hole. Plant freshly purchased bulbs if at all possible, as bulbs that have been stored for a long time can be too dry. Add some organic all-purpose compost to the soil, mixed with a little sand if necessary.

Now mark the position with a little stick, so you know where to expect the shoots. Then plant the next bulb right beside it. Lilies love to be in groups. Maybe they talk to each other in a language we can't understand. They will certainly make a much bigger statement if grown in groups, as their colours are more intense. They will also produce a much headier fragrance en masse, so when choosing a site for them, be sure to leave some space between windows and seating areas, in case everyone does not appreciate their powerful scent.

One more tip: lily bulbs will gladden the heart of any field mice and quickly rob you of your pleasure by becoming mouse food. A good way to prevent this happening is to set up a wire mesh around the bulbs that will keep mice away but not stop the roots from spreading. You can even buy special plastic baskets made just for this purpose.

In many gardens, spring planting of perennials is preferred, as the young plants have plenty of time to develop right through until winter.

This border of tulips, daffodils and hyacinths (left) is a classic, with its vibrant colours of red, yellow and blue. Yellow forsythia flowers are always a sure sign of the first flush of spring (right).

THE ROCKERY—PLANNING AND PLANTING

For lovers of alpine flora, this is the time to plan and plot a rockery. As there are so many suitable annuals, climbers, perennials and grasses, you will be spoilt for choice. Selecting the spot is not a problem. Slopes, terraces and garden walls are equally suitable terrain and you can separate plants with anything from pebbles to boulders.

The threadlike shoots of the Kenilworth ivy pictured here tend to take root quickly. This makes them an ideal choice for providing a rapidly extending green cover, for example on surfaces like stone walls.

Although you will have already prepared the ground for your rockery back in late autumn, the snow, rain and the spring thaw will have since made soil fall between rocks and cracks. Now you will have some beautiful corners and niches in which to install your favourite plants. Before putting any in the ground, however, it pays to have a plan or even a drawing of how you want to your rockery landscape to look.

It's important to bear in mind that rockeries have two big flowering periods that should each be maximised to their full extent: the spring show and the summer spectacle. The perennials and shrubs for spring flowering that you plant now, of course, will not bloom until next year, but you will be able to enjoy some of the summer flowering types yet this year. As you create your rockery design, don't forget to designate some space for autumn planting, too—especially for bulbs and tubers.

ing perennials for early and high summer; flowering bulbs and erica bushes all year round. Shrubs will make the strongest statements, so they should be allocated space first. Small, low-growing conifers and deciduous plants are well suited. Then come the perennials, each of which has its preferred growing conditions. Try to co-ordinate the flowering time, growth pattern and colour of the various plants with one another. Decorative grasses form a very important element of any rockery, and steppe or alpine grasses are particularly effective.

The rockery is not really a heath or moor garden, but some erica plants (there are 50 different varieties in all), look particularly good in a rockery—not only the striking spring-flowering azaleas, but also the small herb-like plants. Winter heath (*Erica carnea*), for instance, flowers from February onwards and adds a chink of pink and red between the rocks.

Heather varieties generally like sunny positions with a suitably moist soil, which in rockeries can be generated by a trickling stream or a rivulet of water. The winter heath is also a ground-hugging plant, reaching only 15 cm (6 in) in height, and thrives in a chalky soil. It looks particularly good in front of chunky rocks and conifers.

Plant heathers in groups to form different coloured clumps of colour as they add a little zing to your rockery. Broom, another spring flowering plant with a bright yellow flower, may temporarily steal the show of the flowering heathers, but later forms a wonderful dark green backdrop to smaller rockery plants.

When building a stone wall, it is important to make sure it is not only stabile, but also has adequate drainage.

When designing a rockery on the scale shown below, you will need to draw up a thorough plan and allow plenty of time and patience for it to develop.

What are the essential components of an attractive rockery? Rocks, naturally, casually dispersed, staggered to form steps or piled up as rock walls. This basic "frame" then needs covering, and the following are all suitable options: low-growing annuals, both flowering and evergreen; flower-

COMPOSTING

A good soil cannot be underestimated if you want to be a successful gardener. The fertility of any soil is directly dependent on the conversion of dead organic material by micro-organisms into nutrients. This kind of humus formation also takes place in concentrated form in your compost bin.

Compost bins are available in all shapes and sizes—yours doesn't have to be a deluxe thermo-composter to be a success. With a little handyman skill, a simple silo for composting organic material can be built by any home gardener.

Whether you use a drum, a wooden bin or a simple pile, compost is easy to create if you observe a few basic rules. Many people are reluctant to set up a compost heap. Some worry about the smell, while others don't like the look of them, but these concerns are not well-founded. There is a suitable spot for a compost heap in almost every garden, where it won't be noticeable and will blend well into the garden. Please do leave a gap between your compost and the neighbour's pro-perty or you may raise some eyebrows, though a well-kept compost heap will not stink at all.

Once you have experienced the benefits of such a simple recycling facility in your own garden, you will be loathe to give up this opportunity to create your own plant food by rotting both kit-chen and garden waste. It also reduces the household rubbish you accumulate. A simple compost heap takes up the most space, with a width of 1.5 metres (5 ft) and a height and length of about 1 metre (3 ft).

The process will work more quickly in a practical thermo-composter. These lockable devices are heated, and the warmth accelerates the rotting process considerably. Raw material for your private humus factory is readily available all year round. For the bottom layer you need normal soil, so that natural soil dwellers like worms can wriggle inside. Next comes coarse material like branches and twigs from your spring pruning, or the shoots and stalks of shrubs. These larger bits and pieces keep the air circulating through the bottom of your compost and prevent it from going mouldy.

On top of this layer place rotting or already rotted compost, which is also available for purchase. However, it is sufficient to just use some earth mixed with compost accelerator and moistened if necessary. A liquid brew made from shredded stinging nettles is the preferred option. At that point your compost container is ready to receive all kinds of organic waste. Once a layer of about 20 to 30 cm (8–12 in) has accumulated you should add some more compost or pre-mixed earth.

What kinds of things can be composted? Garden waste, of course, like leaves, grass clippings, shoots and stalks from trees and shrubs, dead flowers, old soil from pots you have repotted—all of which must be free of any pests or diseases. The other half comes from your kitchen waste, including eggshells, tired-looking fruit and vegetables, tea leaves and coffee grounds. Wilted cut flowers and flowerpots made of natural fibres are both good additions to compost.

Not suitable for composting are fish, cheese and meat remnants, as these promote the dreaded "stink" factor. They will also attract animals. Equally unsuitable are printed paper, the contents of your vacuum cleaner bag, rotten fruit, cabbage stalks (often disease carriers), or food scraps containing preservatives. Inorganic material obviously has no place in a compost bin. Horse manure is a good addition to the compost heap. The faeces of dogs, cats or for that matter, humans, should never be added to the compost pile as they can spread disease.

Rubbish in compost bins generally rots in six to nine months, or three months in a rapid composter. By then humus will have formed. While it is rotting there is no need to turn it, unless it has begun to smell. But if you follow the above guidelines, smell should not be a problem.

Make sure the compost heap doesn't dry out. You may need to water it from time to time, but it should never get too wet, so it is a good idea to cover it during a prolonged spell of rain. Occasionally poking air holes in with a stick will stimulate the rotting process. Before using well-rotted compost in your garden, pass it through a sieve or screen to filter out any large lumps. These can form the start of a new compost heap.

Shredded stinging nettle brew (above) adds valuable minerals to the rotting material. As with all garden preparations, store it carefully away from children and pets.

Compost additives help to speed up the process of rotting your kitchen and garden waste (left).

61

Lawns require not only careful planning before their creation, but also constant maintenance, in order to be able to speak of a "green oasis" in your garden.

LAWN CARE

Lawns are not only easy on the eye, they also have to withstand a lot of wear and tear, so they need to be well looked after. They are not just a collection of grass stalks but, when planted properly, will form a continuous carpet that will not object to children playing on it. Spring is the time to give lawns a good working over.

Spring is also the right time to lay any new lawns. First remove any unwanted weeds from the chosen area and loosen up the soil. Depending on its composition, you may need to add sand or peat to the soil along with other organic matter. On no account sow any lawn seed on a firm, clay soil. It will not store any water and the seed will burn in the first heat of the summer. Roll the prepared soil well and then level it off so you have a nice even surface with no bumps. This will make mowing the lawn much easier later on.

What seed to use? That depends on what the lawn is intended for, its location and the time you have to devote to its care. There are seeds on the market for special purposes like slow-growing lawn or shady lawn. Sometimes the right one for your needs is available, but if not, a mixture may be the ideal solution.

You can sow a lawn by hand or—preferably— with a seed machine. As a rule of thumb, use about 25 grams (1 ounce) of lawn seed per square metre (10 square ft), adding a little more around the edges. Sunny days with little wind are ideal for sowing grass, as less seed will fly away while you are sowing and later when you lightly rake over the area. Tread the seed or roll it in and keep the area well watered.

If you are in a hurry, ready-rolled turf or instant lawn is a possibility. It also saves on the time-consuming business of preparing the soil. You can test the quality of it by its feel. Make sure that the rolls of turf have not been cut off too close to the surface of the root stock, or you may have problems getting it to take root. Ready-roll turf is also suitable for repairing damaged sections of your lawn.

Last year's lawn will need its first trim of the year, after it has been carefully scarified of any moss and dead material. If you are reluctant to buy a scarifying machine you can always hire one. How often you should mow your lawn depends on the circumstances. It is partly a matter of taste and partly determined by the fact that lawn grows at different speeds depending on its location, climate and the type of grass. Every two weeks is about the minimum to ensure the turf develops good stability. The lawn should be about 4 cm (1½ in) high after mowing in the first year, but in subsequent years about 3 cm (1 in) will be sufficient.

New lawn is a very hungry beast, so to begin with you will need to apply some special lawn fertiliser. Later on you can use a special lawn top dressing (which also inhibits moss) several times a year, as required, or a similar product. Some lawns survive quite well without fertiliser but none will thrive for very long without good ventilation. Damp lawn tends to become mossy or develop bald spots.

Real lawn buffs swear by aerification, which is the same thing as ventilation or scarification. There are various machines to do the job, involving pointed iron rakes that dig little holes into the lawn and throw pieces of turf back onto the lawn. This creates a close-knit network of holes of up to 400 indentations per square metre (10 square ft). Then you sprinkle over sand that falls into the holes, allowing water and nutrients to be more easily absorbed by the grass.

A practical tip for lawn lovers is to create a solid border around the edge of your paths or garden beds, as this makes mowing much easier. If a permanent edge looks too severe, you will have to cut your lawn edges frequently so the grass does not grow too tall along the fringes. These days you can buy good edge clippers—some of which are rather noisy but very effective.

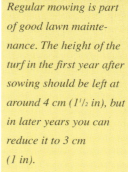

Regular mowing is part of good lawn maintenance. The height of the turf in the first year after sowing should be left at around 4 cm (1½ in), but in later years you can reduce it to 3 cm (1 in).

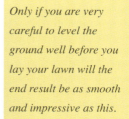

Only if you are very careful to level the ground well before you lay your lawn will the end result be as smooth and impressive as this.

MAY

The beginning of the great flower show also marks the return of the insect world to the garden. The presence of insects is a basic prerequisite for ecological balance and also an excellent method of plant protection.

THE GREAT FLOWER SHOW

When everything is sprouting and many plants are flowering, it's also peak season for pests and weeds. Before these uninvited guests take over, certain measures—preferably ecologically sound ones—have to be taken to protect your vegetable and flower garden from the damage that pests inflict.

These plants that enter our gardens uninvited tend to be much stronger and invade more space than any freshly planted vegetable and flower seedlings. To ensure that your plants are not totally overgrown or suffocated, you will have to do some regular hoeing. This is a good idea anyway, especially in dry spells, since it allows the soil to more efficiently absorb moisture in the air.

Overnight it can still be very cool in May, which adds moisture to the garden, but also presents the added problem of drafts. Sensitive seedlings are vulnerable enough without this, but the wind is generally accompanied by greenfly and blackfly, so plants that prefer warm temperatures should be kept under cover until about mid May. Of course, this is only a general rule of thumb, but it has often proven to be sound advice.

You now have plenty to do in your flower garden. The old flower stalks of any bulbs that have finished flowering should be trimmed, but the leaves should be left in place until they wilt. Adding new compost now will bolster their next flowering season. Older peony roses will also need some fertiliser, and an all-purpose organic compost is best. This is the time to plant new peonies, but don't expect too much from them in the

first year. These plants take a few years to develop fully, but some last for years and years.

It is also time to plant any annuals still on your windowsills or in the greenhouse. Overcast days are best for this, as full sun can be too much of a good thing for young flowers; they need time to adjust to their new surroundings. You can even use an artificial sunshade.

gloves, dahlias and gladioli. Potted plants can go outside in May, too: fuchsias and oleander, citrus trees, cacti and azaleas.

Amidst all the blooming, don't forget the lawn. After all, it provides a green backdrop for the colourful show. It needs at least two May trims because it grows quickly when fertilised. Mowing always draws nutrients from the lawn.

Apple blossoms followed by pear blossoms, lilac and other flowering plants are a sure sign that spring is in full swing in your garden.

Even without strategic planning, a colourful sea of flowers can light up a spring meadow.

Your flower garden will by now be tempting you to take some cut flowers inside. There's nothing better than a big vase full of lilac from your own garden, but be careful to cut flowers with a long, diagonal cut and remove the leaves, as they need too much water and will reduce the amount of moisture the flowers receive. Without direct competition from the leaves you will find flowers last longer, but you can add other greens between the blooms to provide contrast.

The same applies when cutting fruit tree branches, but you won't want to do entirely without leaves as they are so decorative. If you cut off stalks at the bud-forming stage they will bloom beautifully indoors. There are also plenty of things still to be planted in the garden. Annuals and perennials are all worth planting, as well as water and swamp plants, cuttings and seedlings, hollyhocks and fox-

FIRST HARVEST

It's now high season in both the vegetable and flower garden. The last of the early bloomers will be starting to wilt as most perennial flowers and shrubs reach their full summer bloom period. While some sowing may be called for in certain vegetable beds, there will already be plenty to harvest in others with kohlrabi, lettuce, radishes and spinach all ready to pick.

Meanwhile, the vegetable garden should be providing plenty of food in the form of early kohlrabi, lettuce and salad greens, radishes and spinach. White asparagus is considered a delicacy on the Continent and this is the month to plant and pick it. It is slightly milder and nuttier in flavour than green asparagus.

To grow enough white asparagus to be worthwhile you need plenty of space. It's not particularly difficult to grow once you have created the right plot, but it does take time to see any results, as it can be three years before any real crop eventuates. You also need a bed that is a good 12 metres (40 ft) long to produce enough for four people.

Very fertile soil is absolutely vital—neither too wet nor too dry—which is why asparagus is typically grown in raised beds. Ideally it also needs to be grown in quite a sunny spot. Work the soil down to a good depth initially, as

The white asparagus so thoroughly enjoyed on the Continent has its peak season from mid April through to 24 June. Other vegetables are also ready to enjoy this time of year, such as radishes or salad greens.

Let's stay with the vegetable garden, where seed sowing and vegetable planting is now in full swing. This is the time for beans, kale, chicory and winter carrots. Precautionary measures are also advisable in the cauliflower bed, as these vegetables will be approaching maturity next month and may need covering to ensure they stay white. Tomatoes grow very quickly at this time of year and will need to be supported by tying them to stakes.

asparagus has deep roots. Add some well-rotted manure to the furrows and then work some bone meal into the topsoil.

Spring is the time to plant and pick asparagus. Don't buy plants that are too old. It is a fallacy that the older they are, the bigger the crop; one or two year old plants are ideal. On a dry day, break up any clods with your work boots, then form flat furrows about 90 cm (3 ft) apart and mound up a raised bed from the soil you have gained.

Then put in the plants, which have been kept nice and moist, with their root structure hanging over the side of the bed before covering them with soil. Keep individual plants about 50 cm (20 in) apart. When you have finished, the roots should be covered with about 10 cm (4 in) of soil. Apart from adding a little compost now and then, you can leave them to their own devices for two years before it is time to pick your first crop. You will need a sharp knife with a narrow blade to do the job. Slide the knife gently underneath the surface of the mound and cut off each spear when you can see it has formed a good length. Initially you may find harvesting the crop a great deal of fun, as it is so different from the way any other vegetable is picked. It's tricky though, so don't be disappointed if your first results are not very professional.

Meanwhile, in your flower garden it's all go. Late tulip varieties will still be flowering but these will gradually fade into the background. They will start to look quite old by comparison with the typical blooms and flowers of May. There's so much to feast your eyes on, it's easy to forget that there are other plants to consider if you want the colours to keep on coming.

Roses, for instance, will be sprouting furiously at this point and buds will start to appear. It's time to apply the second dose of food in the form of a special rose fertiliser, which should be worked into the soil. If it is dry, make sure you water it well immediately. Sometimes a few wild shoots pop up out of the earth that come from underneath the graft. They will have to be removed. It's best

to pull them out with a quick tug, but gardening gloves are essential for this job.

Gardens at this time of year are brimming with rhododendron blooms and their sisters, the azaleas, will also be in full flower. Both are very thirsty and will not draw enough moisture from the ground during dry periods. Water them well, so as to have the benefit of their beauty for a little longer, and keep removing any deadheads to prolong the show even further.

The ruby-red horse chestnut (top) is one of the more robust ornamental shrubs.

Mid to late blooming tulips like the "Texas Flame" (above) first appear well into May.

THE HERB GARDEN

Herbs are both decorative and edible. Even half-hearted cooks will come to appreciate their uses in a very short space of time, and anyone who has ever planted them is convinced of their decorative appeal. Besides which, the savoury fragrance of dill or thyme in the air adds a touch of flair to any garden.

Many gardeners like to add clusters of herbs to various garden plots. The once common practice of keeping them in a separate herb garden was based on a desire to keep track of them all, as the healing power of their seeds and extracts—along with their culinary properties—were the main focus of attention. Herbs for the kitchen and first aid purposes should be kept close at hand. Now with pills available for every purpose, we have come to appreciate herbs' decorative function and the uplifting atmosphere they create.

This is why lavender is often found between roses, summer savoury in the rockery and mint around the garden pond. Herbs still belong in the vegetable garden, of course, as they often add flavour to vegetable dishes and stewed fruits. When you go to pick a cucumber, it's natural to glance at your dill clump and, in your mind's eye, you're already preparing a delicious salad.

Almost all herbs need sun, but some like dry, limy conditions while others prefer a moist, humus-rich soil to fully develop their aromas. They are otherwise easy to look after, need no or only occasional fertiliser and are quite compatible with most small animals. It's not advisable to use pest control products in the herb garden.

Classic herbs (from top to bottom and left to right): lavender, marjoram, woodruff, sage, tarragon and lovage.

Here are some tips on harvesting your herbs. They should be dry when you pick them. Do not pick herbs during rainy weather or when dew is on the ground. The hot midday sun is also inappropriate, as the concentration of essential oils that carry the aromas are at their lowest ebb. For this reason they should not be washed after cutting, but simply rinsed off beforehand with the watering can, left to dry and then cut. Herbs contain the highest concentration of valuable nutrients just before flowering. Any cut herbs can be hung in an airy, but shady place to dry. Drying them in the sun unnecessarily robs them of much of their aroma. If the dried stalks rustle to the touch, then your herbs are "ready". This makes it easier to pluck off the leaves and chop them finely. Kept in an airtight jar they will retain their flavour for a long time.

Now let's take a brief look at three very important herbs.

Tarragon: The plant has an aromatic fragrance, grows up to 120 cm (4 ft) in height and can be planted from seed now, or even earlier in humus-rich soil. Once seedlings appear they can be transplanted about 40 cm (15 in) apart and kept well watered. It pays to stake the plants as they are susceptible to wind. Tarragon has narrow green leaves and produces a whitish/green flower in late summer. This herb is best cut and dried before it blooms. Rub the small leaves together to add the desired flavour to pickled gherkins, salads, sauces and mayonnaise.

Marjoram: This aromatic herb is one of the most popular of all. Marjoram is often raised from seed in a pot or cold frame and then transplanted in May about 30 cm (12 in) apart. At this time of year seeds can also be planted out in the open. The plant, which grows up to 50 cm (18 in) tall, has small elliptical leaves with a grey, velvety surface. It will grow into a bushy, broad plant. It's best to harvest the twigs at the budding stage and before they flower, if possible. Poultry, meatloaf, sausage dishes, potato recipes and sauces all benefit from the distinctively pleasant aroma of this herb. Taken as a tea, marjoram can also offer relief from colic.

Sage: Botanists recognise over 700 varieties of sage; garden sage is the most common. It contains a high concentration of essential oils and is also a popular decorative plant. It grows to 70 cm (27 in) high, has a particularly aromatic fragrance, long, pointed grey/green leaves with a wrinkly, velvety feel and a purple flower. As a healing plant, sage is useful for colds, inflammation and breathing problems. In the kitchen it is particularly good in pork, liver and eel dishes.

Herbs are not only valued for their culinary properties—many herbs can also be used for healing purposes, so by growing them you can create your own little pharmacy in the garden.

BALCONY PLANTS

A balcony full of plants is not always a sign that space is at a premium. It's often motivated by the desire to soften bare walls or clad them with natural colour. Particularly in the merry month of May, vertical gardening can be a very rewarding pastime. Geraniums, fuchsias and African marigolds are some of the most well known, but by no means all, of the balcony options.

There's a long tradition of cultivating plants in containers, particularly on the Continent, where only a few people have the luxury of spacious garden settings.

As wonderful as balconies look at this time of year, with the bounties of nature all flowering at their peak, there are a few ground rules for decorating the front of your house. In choosing plants, think about how they will look against the backdrop of the wall or the roof above. What are you trying to achieve? Privacy for yourself or a good show of colour for others? Whatever you decide, make sure you choose a mixture that will give you lasting pleasure.

One man's meat is another man's poison, as the saying goes, and the same applies here. Not everyone will share your taste and the tenant below you may not appreciate your watering can dribbling onto her breakfast table.

If you are not the owner of the house, your landlord might well take exception to your luxuriant wall hangings. Climbing plants, for instance, can leave unsightly traces on the plasterwork, and dripping water also leaves its mark. Too many containers and pots can become a dangerous hobby. A freshly watered flowerpot can hold a great deal of weight and too many large tubs can play havoc with the structural engineering of your balcony.

A basic premise is, when you're working on your balcony, always remember who's down below. Gravity is definitely a factor in gardening, so check all fixtures to make sure your flower tubs don't topple over the edge. Over time, even wrought iron will shows signs of wear, wood can go rotten and screws become loose. Before planting, check which direction your balcony faces, too. That will help you choose which plants are best suited to the spot. Geraniums, for instance, love full sun; begonias and marigolds thrive on east and west-facing balconies; while fuchsias and Busy Lizzie (impatiens) will be content with a north-facing site.

Good gardeners don't just know their plants—they want them to give pleasure to themselves and others. This can happen all year round if you make the right planting choices, as even in winter there are evergreens and other colourful options to choose from. In May, balcony gardeners, like backyard exponents, are spoilt for choice.

The classic balcony plant is still the pelargonium, commonly know as the geranium. There are endless cultivars to choose from. The ivy geranium is the most common and also comes in a number of different shapes and sizes. The Balcon series of cultivars is popular and make a cascading display in reds, pinks or striking salmon, whichever you choose. 'Amethyst' is an outstanding member of this series, with lilac pink flowers. The shoots of these plants hang well down, so they are ideal for balconies and hanging baskets. All geraniums are frost-sensitive, so they are generally planted after mid May when there is less risk of frost occurring.

Geraniums need plenty of water. As balconies in high-rise buildings are often overshadowed by other balconies or roofs, your flowers may not get enough rainwater, so regular watering is required, even if it rains. Container plants also need good nutrients, so regular compost is an essential addition. Geraniums planted out at this time of year will continue flowering until early autumn if you remove any deadheads, and they can be stored in a dry cellar over the winter.

Perhaps geraniums are too pedestrian and you would rather have something different for a change. If so, you can concoct some stunning colour combinations—tone-on-tone or in striking contrasts. Yellow shades of shrub verbena, delicate white alyssum, the charming Mt Atlas daisy and Mexican daisy (fleabane) all convey a sense of lightness, while a mix of orange zest salvia, fuchsias, ornamental tobacco and lobelia will produce a blaze of colour.

A whole tub of marigolds can also provide a colourful composition, as this member of the *Tagetes* family comes in all different shapes, sizes and markings. You can even get multi-coloured marigolds and some with double blooms. The colours range from bright yellow to

a vivid reddish-orange. If you don't want your flower box to be too overpowering, try the smaller *Tagetes tenuifolia* "Lemon Gem" that is also suitable for planting at this time of year.

Lobelias, slipper flowers, verbenas, Bellis daisy cultivars and Busy Lizzie can also be used to good effect. It's all a question of the interplay of colours and greenery, colour on colour or the contrast between backdrop and plants. There's no façade so perfect that it can't be enhanced by decorative flowers or climbing plants.

Of course, edible plants such as salad greens, radishes, tomatoes, herbs and other vegetables can also be grown in window boxes, containers or conservatories and contribute much to the overall appeal of any balcony.

Geraniums are still considered one of the classic balcony plants.

Balcony planting does not have to be limited to a few containers. You can suspend some hanging baskets to break up the line and create a garden on several levels (above).

A FLOWERING MEADOW

Formal lawn or flowering meadow—one of the difficult decisions to make in designing any garden. Lawns are certainly more work and can appear a bit monotonous. In the plus column, a lawn will cope with a lot more than any meadow can handle. A flowering meadow, on the other hand, is more pleasing to the eye and attracts wildlife into the garden.

Although strictly linear lawns may be an ideal that many garden owners strive for, summer meadows exude a picture of fresh colour and opulent abundance.

Perhaps the children have grown up and things have become more sedate in the garden. When there's no longer any need to have a lawn for kids to play on, many people in this situation decide to save themselves the bother and opt for an informal meadow instead. Meadows are more attractive than green grass and also bring in the butterflies and dragonflies, beetles and bees. Prospective meadow gardeners see themselves tearing up the lawn, sowing some wildflower seeds and sitting back to watch the grass grow interspersed with buttercups and spring foxgloves.

Would that it were so easy. Lawns, in fact, grow on the kind of rich soil that meadows do not thrive on. If your close-cropped green is ever to be transformed into a colourful forest of informal flowers, the former lawn will have to undergo a new diet first. That can't begin until you've drastically reduced the amount of mowing, and immediately removed any clippings, so the soil is not too moist. While wildflowers will happily sprout, they won't last long in a lawn environment because the little blooms won't stand a chance against a thick carpet of grass. The kind of herbs you used to think of as weeds when you kept a manicured lawn are more likely to survive: dandelions and marguerites, daisies and small buttercups. However, it will still take them a good while to turn your lawn into a wild meadow. The piece of land in question will not look particularly attractive in the interim, so it may be better to remove the whole turf (if it's not too big an area), and prepare the kind of soil that meadows really prefer.

Meadow flower seeds can only be directly sown onto a soil that is low in nutrients. If you used to have a lawn where the informal meadow is destined to go, the ground will still be too rich in the lower regions. For this reason, it's a good

idea to bring in some barren soil mixed with sand to apply to the dug up ground where the turf used to be, until the old level surface is restored. If you want to end up with a dry meadow, the ground will have to be very sandy or even stony to succeed.

Usually a damper kind of meadow is preferred, as it tends to produce more colourful flowers. Your taste alone will not necessarily determine the final result, as location is also crucial. On a sunny, wind-protected slope you will have no choice but to go for a dry meadow, while a nearby stream will steer you clearly in the direction of a marshy meadow. You can buy the desired seed mix in any garden shop (usually one third grass, one third flowers), including ones that contain wild forms of edible plants like wild sorrel or watercress. Different grasses look good in a wild meadow too, like yellow oat grass and quaking grass or creeping red fescue. May is exactly the right month to sow seed, as you will see the first results, however modest, in the same year and you will be able to harvest some in autumn. The following year you can mow the meadow twice: once after the spring flowering and again after your summer plants have gone to seed again.

No other work is required. Regeneration or propagation occurs through the natural environment itself, as birds bring in seed and the wind blows it about. This brings us to a potential problem. If you live in a residential area, your meadow may not meet with universal approval. Some lawn lovers will be afraid of inheriting weeds from your natural habitat, so you may have to take steps to keep neighbours happy. No meadow is worth stirring up a hornet's nest in an otherwise peaceful suburban setting.

Even daisies and dandelions can conjure up the flair of a wild meadow (left).

Marguerites and wild salvias form the basis of a diverse and ecologically rich habitat (below).

JUNE

MIDSUMMER HARVEST

In June the first fruits and all kinds of homegrown vegetables make up for all the work now required in the garden. Pests need to be eradicated, roses looked after, hedges trimmed and lawns mowed, but the growing amount of tasty produce from your vegetable and fruit garden should be more than adequate compensation for your efforts.

The flowers of the meadow foxtail are one of the signs that let farmers know that it's time to start harvesting the hay from their fields. In your flower garden, the first summer flowers can be cut back and deadheads and shoots removed.

Let's begin by tackling garden pests. Weeding or hoeing are essential, of course, but there are other ways to get rid of greedy little critters that don't involve too many chemicals or cause environmental problems. It's really worthwhile using ecologically sound options for pest control.

A few traditional household remedies demonstrate that some plants are up to the job of warding off little beasts. Take the age-old use of stinging nettle or field horsetail, garlic or wormwood. These insect repellents are also available in dried form, but it takes some effort to "prepare" them. As with any pest control, store it out of reach of children and pets. To protect your cultivated plants with a spray, we recommend the following: stinging nettle brew as a remedy against pea leaf weevils, aphids, whitefly, greenfly, bird cherry ermine, potato beetle, spider mites and cherry fruit flies. Take 1 kg (2 lbs) of nettle (the leaves and stems, cut before it flowers) or 200 g (7 oz) dried nettle, soak it well in 10 litres (2 gallons) rain water for four to five days, and leave in the sun to ferment until the brew is light and foamy. Dilute 1:10 in a watering can and spray onto leaves and shoots. By the way, any unused brew that darkens in colour makes great liquid compost, also diluted 1:10.

June is the month for sun-ripened straw-berries, the berry the ancient Greeks called "Queen of all Fruits".

When all the flowers, perennials and shrubs start to show their colours in early summer, you need to keep an eye out for potential pests and predators like the ever-present aphid.

A similar brew can be made of horsetail. It is an effective means of warding off fungal infections like black spot, grey mould, white pine blister rust, club root in cabbages, potato blight, vine mildew and the grass disease "brown patch". It also needs to be applied several days in a row to achieve the best results.

Wormwood tea is effective against aphids, pea moths, cabbage white butterflies, apple sawflies and spider mites. Undiluted garlic tea is the first method of attack against carrot root fly and strawberry spider mite. A dusting of lime sulphur spray fights off ants, striped flea beetle, potato beetle, cabbage fly, blights affecting brassica and potatoes, and onion fly. Armed with this spray, you won't need to worry about your roses, which are now in full bloom and tend to become infected with mildew. If so, treat as above. However, when it comes to the dreaded black spot, you will probably need to resort to stronger fungicides. You can take some preventative action by allowing generous spaces between individual rose plants and avoiding water logging of the soil.

Hedges are preferable to any artificial wind blocks or other structures as a structural element or border. They do require regular trimming, and by June broad-leaved shrubs are well due for their first cut. Hedges grown from young plants should be cut right back so they develop good spurs and thicken well. They will grow up to a good 20 cm (8 in) a year. Remember, too, that even hedges need watering in dry weather.

June is also the time for sweet treats. Cherries will be starting to ripen, but the real harvest of the month is strawberries. If the plants have been well watered and fed, you will enjoy some very flavoursome fruit this time of year. Always pick them in the morning by separating ripe fruit from the plant such that the hull remains in the berry, as they keep better that way. It also stops them from "bleeding" when you wash them.

After harvesting, strawberries will produce runners. Select the healthiest of them and allow them to grow. The rest of the runners should be removed so they don't place an unnecessary drain on the plant.

CUT FLOWERS

The longest days of the year will see an extraordinary wealth of perennials and shrubs in full bloom. Your flower garden will be in its glory, so it's the ideal time to bring some of the splendour inside. Gladioli, dahlias and calendulas or garden marigolds are a sure sign that it's cut flower time.

non-hardy varieties or modern hybrids cultivated in glasshouses and propagated by bulb division are more common these days. Many of these ornamental gladioli have elegant two-coloured blooms, with white or amber predominating. Blue and finely marked or speckled varieties are also popular, but the deep reds stand out most of all.

Big bunches of gladioli in three or more colours add a great dash of summer to any room. Be careful when cutting them not to remove all the leaves, as the bulbs will suffer and produce much weaker specimens the following year. However, if you keep planting out new ones every year anyway, you might as well add the leaves to your indoor flower arrangements. Beautiful, though smaller, bouquets can be made of garden dahlias that will bloom over and over again all through the summer. The tall varieties are particularly popular as cut flowers. Their

Country gardens put on a great display in early summer. Gladioli are often prominently featured in such gardens, with their elegant, funnel-shaped flowers that come in an immense variety of colours and shapes.

Let's choose a particularly gratifying cut flower from the profusion on offer at this time of year—the gladiolus. In warm and sunny spots around your garden, gladioli will be in full bloom in June. New cultivars now offer more impressive colours than ever before. Their name, which comes from the Latin *gladius* ("sword"), marks them as belonging to the iris family. Gladioli are also known as sword lilies, though the only thing remotely combative about them is the stalwart length of their flowering time. Their flowers are arranged along the length of the stem and open one after another, extending the bright show these plants make in the garden a good while.

With their bulbous roots, many will survive the winter, like the *Gladiolus communis* or southern European species, with its rich magenta blooms, which can grow up to 1 metres (3 ft) high. The

blooms grow as big as 9 cm (3½ in) and come in orange-red ('Dompfaff'), scarlet red ('Nelly Geerings'), pure white ('Sneezy') or dark velvety red ('Zons'). They need more care in a container than they do in the ground, but are constantly thirsty anyway, due to their large leaves. Regular watering also helps prevent an attack of greenfly.

You won't see anything of the biennials you sow this season until next year. Most of them are winter hardy. They will germinate in early autumn. At this time you can sow or plant them in their allotted place and rely upon them to be very decorative by next spring or summer. Sweet William and thrift, garden forget-me-nots, sweet rocket and wallflowers all make June a particularly beautiful month.

Sow seeds in a shady place where there is no danger of the soil drying out too quickly. The seedlings that emerge should be pricked out or not placed too close together as seeds. Once you have transplanted them into your flowerbeds, water them regularly.

There is one other thing to note on the ornamental front for next year. At the end of the month you will be able to take out your spring

flowering bulbs, once the foliage has died off. Tulip bulbs should be removed every year, while daffodils can be left in the ground for years. For cut flowers you should separate the new shoots from the mother bulb and plant them in fresh soil. This also applies if the bulbs produce leaves. Here's how to take them out: dig a spade well into the soil so it goes underneath the bulbs. Then pull out the bulbs and shake off the earth. Then they have to be dried. The best way is to place them in low containers with a base of mesh or wire netting. An airy shed is ideal for storing them. Label the bulbs by type so it is easier to plant them out again next time. Don't remove any dead foliage from the bulbs until it is completely dry. The same applies to the roots and the skin of the bulb itself. Throw away any wrinkled, overly small or rotten bulbs. As they can be carriers of diseases or germs, they should not end up the compost.

Here is one more tip worth noting. There is a way to encourage hardy perennials that have already flowered to bloom again in autumn: cut them back severely. Among the flowers that respond well to such radical treatment are delphiniums, daisies, purple cone flowers and European globe flowers.

The marigold, which flowers from June to October, is one of the oldest ornamental cultivars for flower gardens.

With the flaming colour of its leaves and abundant fruit, the stag horn sumac is in full bloom around June or July.

PEAS, CARROTS AND LETTUCE

It's harvest time in the vegetable garden. Apart from peas, carrots and lettuce, this is also the month for cauliflower, broad beans, swede, radish and dill as well as plenty of other fresh produce. In addition to harvesting all these the garden still needs to be tended and the the continuation of your success assured by planting and sowing anew.

cabbage. It is also time to bed down leeks, root celery and courgette in their outdoor spots.

Some late vegetables must be sown from seed, like chicory. Bear in mind that some seeds germinate under sand or a light covering of soil, while others need light to germinate. Chicory is a popular leafy vegetable you can harvest twice. In June, sow the cultivated form in rows in not too rich soil and plant it out after germination at 15-cm (6-in) intervals. You can cut off the leaves about 3 cm (1 in) above the root in October and add them to salads.

You can then blanch the chicory by digging up the leaf-less plants and planting them in pots or boxes. Take them inside and let them grow in a dark place. You can make tasty salads from the white leaves in winter.

Companion planting is about "good neighbours", i.e. a mix of compatible species that have a positive effect on one another when close together in the same plot, such as strawberries with onions (above).

Sowing in rows is the most common method in the vegetable garden. The distance between rows depends on the space each type of vegetable needs, but is generally 20 to 40 cm (8–16 in).

Of course there's still plenty to be done. How could it be otherwise in the month of greatest growth? Sadly, unwanted plants are also having a growth spurt, so weeding is high on the agenda. Of course watering is important, too. The impending summer means beautiful, but dry, days are upon us. It's best to decide in the evening how much or indeed whether to water the garden at all. A shower of cold tap water in the midday sun can give vegetables that prefer warmth, like beans, cucumbers and tomatoes, a nasty shock.

Even if you're busy harvesting, you will still get a lot of pleasure from new plantings. Nothing succeeds like success, and you'll want to pick and trim, cut and harvest all kind of produce in the coming months. Late vegetables should go in the ground now, from your own seedlings or a garden shop. This includes late brassicas such as kale and kohlrabi (the first crop will have been picked earlier), Brussels sprouts and drumhead

Vegetable gardens are not merely a source of vitamins: they also provide much pleasure to the gardener, combining a beloved occupation with a sense of achievement and superior freshness and flavour.

Radicchio, the Italian form of chicory with distinctive red leaves (thanks to the pigment anthrocyanin), is also due for planting, but not before about 20 June. In autumn the leaves (minus the heart!) will produce a hearty salad. After that, the plant will form red heads that can be harvested until winter starts. Should any snow or frost intervene, cover them with twigs for adequate protection. Another note on thrifty vegetable gardening: if you don't use all of your turnips straight away, they can be stored in a dark, cool, dry place perfectly well for quite some time.

Courgettes are very popular now. This green, or sometimes yellow striped, pumpkin variety grows rapidly and needs a huge amount of space. To ensure they don't overcrowd other vegetables, plant courgettes on and near your compost heap, where it will not compete with other plants. This will allow them to feed to their heart's content. Just one or two plants produce enough for the whole family.

Plant out seedlings through mid June. They need frequent watering and protection from snails. Other pests are not interested in courgettes, so you won't need to spray them. They do like stinging nettle brew, more as fertiliser than a pest control method. After just five to six weeks you may be able to pick your first crop. Go ahead and take them as soon as they form, as this encourages the plant to produce more flowers and new courgettes will follow.

PEST CONTROL

The bounty of fruit and vegetables that accompany this month's abundance unfortunately attract more than gardeners to the garden. Maggots, greenflies, mites and caterpillars will need to be dealt with—as gently as possible—in the month of June. Butterflies, ladybirds and bees, on the other hand, are very helpful and desirable creatures to have around at this time of year.

Prevention is certainly always better than a cure, but it's not always easy to prevent plants from falling victim to pests, even if you follow the rules carefully. The insects we so despise are living creatures like any other, and only have such a bad reputation because they get in the way of our endeavours. Gardeners traditionally have declared all-out war on them, but these days tend to favour ecological methods, as mentioned earlier in this chapter. Sometimes, however, the biological potions simply don't work and you will have to resort to chemical means.

Whether it's time to take lethal action and which methods should be applied depends on the type and behaviour of each "enemy" you deal with. Try to understand how they behave and work out whether the threat they represent can be counteracted by mechanical means (e.g. removal of caterpillars or preventative measures) or biological ones (encourage their natural enemies into the garden, or use coffee on snails, for instance). When new leaves on a tree are under attack, you can count on renewed growth in June to make up for any losses. Even a light cold snap can do wonders in some cases.

Aphids (above) attack roses, balcony and container plants, while the caterpillars of the bird cherry ermine (below) are capable of enveloping entire plants in their webs.

If you find stronger measures are required after all, take rigorous action but choose a sensible combination of chemical and biological methods. Even when using insecticides (substances that kill both insects and their larvae), a mix of sprays and pellets is recommended, as they each have different effects—short-term poisons work on the surface and long-term killers are taken up by the plant roots. They will kill all sucking and biting insects and will only hurt the plants if not applied properly or used too frequently—in which case they may even encourage the growth of resistant pests.

Always read the instructions on any preparations very carefully and make sure nobody comes into direct contact with the poison. This means using protective clothing (when spraying, for instance) and keeping children and pets well away from the garden you are treating.

The same applies to antifungal products (fungicides). They are usually more important and more effective than insecticides, as the underlying causes of fungal diseases are often very persistent, difficult to locate and hard to eradicate. This is why sulphur-based products or other inorganic fungicides have to be used frequently over a wide area. Organic fungicides are recommended as better options in most cases, since they are programmed to address the particular "enemy" in question.

The use of poison is inadvisable for larger pests like rats. Mechanical devices such as plastic cages to protect bulbs can help in the fight against gnawing pests. Special traps are also preferable to the use of poisonous bait, which is also harmful to humans.

Whitefly (above) is a pest that primarily frequents greenhouses, but is also found in balcony containers or garden beds over the summer.

Greedy slugs (centre) are a nightmare for any gardener.

The water vole or water rat (below left) is a harmless creature in the UK, seldom seen in the garden unless a stream is nearby. Its European cousins, however, cause a great deal of trouble, digging extensive tunnels. Moles' tunnels may be troublesome, but they do eat harmful insects and are even a protected species in some places.

THE GARDEN POND

Even in a small garden, there is always a little corner somewhere for a tiny wetland habitat. The extra flora in the form of aquatic plants and increased fauna as well– from the whirligig beetle to the goldfish—add interest to any garden. It doesn't even take a great deal of effort to set up or maintain one.

> Achieving ecological equilibrium in the garden is becoming increasingly important these days, and garden ponds can help create habitats that are important for the survival of certain species.

No matter how small your garden pond is, put it in the sunniest place possible. Almost all water lilies and most water flowers prefer warmth and are hungry for sunlight. Parked under tall trees or in the shade of the house, you won't have much of your water feature, which can otherwise be an opulent oasis in the garden. With trees you also have the problem of falling leaves, which make the bottom of the pond increasingly mucky and reduce the depth of the water; yet if you remove the sludge too often, you'll disturb the natural balance and biotopes in the water for some time to come.

Let's look at miniature pools a little longer. Ready-made basins that are lowered into the ground are one option. They are available in many sizes and materials, from moderately pro-portioned tubs made of plastic, fibre cement or concrete to some that are quite large. Sloping walls are an obvious necessity, but be sure to leave a shallow ledge of some sort if you wish to use any plants that grow in shallower water. Larger concrete ponds are best constructed on site by experienced trades people. Excavate the ground in graduated layers to produce a more diverse water feature, creating a refuge for fish, frogs or salamanders, with shallower areas for bog or "shore" lovers. If you want to take the do-it-yourself approach, it's best to work with PVC or polythene pond liners. A water feature should last a few decades, so choose a strong sheeting material and seal any joins carefully. You should also make sure that no plants with deep roots are likely to pierce the lining and

cause leaks. Cover the roughly 30-cm (12-in) wide, overlapping lining with soil and/or bricks and stones to ensure it stays put. The kidney shape, consisting of one wide and one narrow section, is a good choice for liner ponds.

Plant the pond by inserting plants directly into the water. Especially decorative are water lilies, which come in varieties for all water depths (these should not be out of water for too long). The very prolific, white flowering 'Nymphaea Alba', for instance, is best for larger ponds and will grow at a depth of 20 to 80 cm (8–30 in). Cinnamon sedge or common mares tail are good for graduating plantings from water to shore level on the narrow side of the pond. At the wider end, bog bean is ideal. Planting around the margins also helps create smooth transitions and blunts hard contours. Grasses like Chinese bamboo also help soften the edges.

Despite attempts to include a range of tall and lower-growing plants, in the interest of a "natural look" broad leaf marsh plants will always be the main feature of small garden ponds. They provide shade at ground level and landing spots for insects like dragonflies, those ingenious creatures that live near water.

The ideal soil mix for aquatic plants is one-third lime and two-thirds peat. Place this in the basin without compost (which can encourage algae to take over). If you discover snails in the water, suppress any instinct to kill them on sight as you would garden slugs. Water snails are essential in any pond, as they remove dead plant material and convert it into nutrients.

You can add aquatic plants to the pond from the first day of spring to late autumn. You can buy seedlings with fully formed root structures in pots. In determining their position in the pond, go by the same rule of thumb that applies to a perennial garden: tall plants for visual effect and wind protection to the back, dwarf varieties to the front. Water lilies belong on the sunniest side if you want their flowers to develop to their full potential and act as beacons to shiny dragonflies and wondering humans alike.

We mentioned fish earlier. Many people are reluctant to include them because they need looking after, but they offer the advantage, like frogs, of preventing your pond from becoming a breeding ground for mosquitoes. Happily for pond owners, fish like to eat mosquitoes. Two basins are ideal for fish, connected by an overflow or plunge pool lined with aquatic plants. This bit of moving water encourages oxygenation, is highly decorative and gives a dynamic touch to any pond.

Ponds for fish and frogs should be up to 1.5 metres (5 ft) deep if they are to overwinter there. All kinds of goldfish are ideal for garden ponds, of course, but sticklebacks, tench and veil tail varieties are also suitable. Don't put too many fish in your pool. The basic rule is two finger-length fish per square metre (10 square ft) of surface area.

Pond liners (left) allow great flexibility in pond design, but prefabricated basins are also a good option, in particular for smaller ponds.

Nitrates are an important nutrient for algae; too much, however, upsets the ecological balance (centre).

A marshy area (below) should be included in any pond.

JULY

CHERRIES, CARROTS AND EARLY POTATOES

You may have already sampled some early cherries in June as a foretaste of your summer fruit crop, but now is the time to pick the juiciest fruit from your trees and berry canes. July is also the month for diligent gardeners to make preparations for other soon-to-be-ripe fruit and vegetables.

Straight after harvesting your delicious sweet cherries is the ideal time to start pruning the trees. The dreaded sap bleed is more likely to occur on cherry trees if you leave pruning of the thicker branches until autumn. Thin out the crown of the trees and cut away any shoots growing too close together or in an inward direction, so later in the year you will have only minimal corrective pruning to attend to.

Sour cherries of the morello variety take a little longer to ripen, but still peak at the height of summer. Once they have been picked it's time to prune them, too. If you wait they will often form whip-like shoots that place an unnecessary drain on the tree and give sour cherries the unjustified reputation of being poor fruit-bearing varieties. Morello cherries bear fruit almost exclusively on last year's wood. This is why it is important to cut back the fruit-bearing spurs immediately

Cherries that come from your neighbour's garden supposedly always taste better than your own. Whether or not that is true, the first ripe stone fruit is certainly an occasion for you to enjoy the fruits of your labours in the most literal sense of the words.

after harvesting—ideally down to the young shoots near lead branches. Treat any larger cut surfaces with a wound dressing or pruning paint. Peaches will not be ripe just yet, but some thinning of the branches will be tolerated. Any earlier in the year could damage a sensitive tree. On no account remove any short, strongly flowering shoots, but you must remove the long, pointed wood buds. The roughly pencil-thick fruitwoods that carry the most fruit in the coming year should be cut back by about a third now, so they can grow with renewed vigour. The general rule is to thin out any rampantly growing shoots directly after harvesting peaches.

In your vegetable garden the soil will be crying out for a work over, as the first crop will have taken its toll. You can take early carrots from the garden now, but leave late maturing varieties in the ground to develop more. Use a hoe or rake to loosen the soil to a good depth. The same applies to potatoes, some of which will be ready to harvest now, while others have to stay underground a bit longer. The early potatoes that taste so delicious and can be enjoyed with their skins on should be used soon after digging. They are not good keepers.

Carrots, like potatoes, need extra compost after the first of them have been picked. The first choice for carrots is organic all-purpose compost, but without manure that could attract pests.

Potatoes will thank you for green manuring. This biological method of working fast-growing plants into the soil improves fertility by adding air and vitality to the soil, making the sod finer and increasing nitrogen levels. Green manure plants are sown directly in the garden bed between existing plants and later worked into the soil while still green or flowering.

July is the time for intensive soil work in the garden. Your efforts will be rewarded, as most plants only thrive on a good base.

In your garden pond the main problem at this time of year is probably curbing excessive plant growth rather than adding any new specimens. It's a good idea, for instance, to thin out any rampant white water-buttercup.

PERENNIALS

Herbaceous perennials are robust and prolific bloomers in the summer, but they still need care and attention—especially when in full bloom. They are not particularly sensitive if you neglect them every now and again, but if you want to continue appreciating their many charms, don't leave them too long unattended.

Legend has it that it was during the Middle Ages that the first flowers and plants were introduced into gardens that were valued for reasons other than their usefulness. If these tales are true, we have the medieval love of beauty to thank for the importation of peony roses, marigolds and daffodils, as well as the delphiniums that grace so many of today's flower gardens.

Perennials will happily go on producing new blooms, but only if you remove the deadheads. In fact, such attention will encourage many perennials to develop their full beauty. They will also thank you for removing any weeds that have crept in amongst them, as this allows them to absorb more nutrients. In the summer holiday month of July there are often quite large intervals between weeding sessions, as it's hard to find anyone to help out—let alone someone who will do a good job. So it can happen that uninvited guests thrive to the point of flowering themselves and developing seeds. To prevent weeds from self-sowing, cut seed heads and flowers into a bag before weeding out the plants themselves. Otherwise, when you pull them out with a vengeance they will scatter their fertile booty all over the flowerbed.

One of the symbols of summer is lavender, which starts flowering at this time of year and continues through October. This perennial needs the kind of dry, well-drained soil it enjoys in its Mediterranean homeland. Your thanks for treating it well—cutting it back in spring and removing any dried material—will be a sea of violet and a heady fragrance redolent of summer.

You can bring lavender inside as well. Try cutting bunches and allowing them to dry. They'll reward you with the scent of summer when the season is long gone. Tips taken from new shoots can be used to grow new plants. Place cuttings in a seedling tray with a sand/peat mixture and keep in a warm and shady place. Take the plants inside if it gets too cold outside and always keep them moist, leaving them over the winter in a cool but frost-free environment.

A water garden is the ideal place to be on hot summer days. The humming of insects is as much a part of the soothing atmosphere as the yellow splodges of colour from pond lily flowers perched between large, plate-sized leaves. Not as showy as the actual water lily, this easy-going aquatic plant makes an impact with the sheer number of its flowers and its ability to keep its head above water. It even thrives in semi-shaded areas.

Create a frame for your water feature by planting around the edges with reeds and canary grass, but only if your pond is big enough. You need to leave some gaps, as the grass can reach substantial heights in full midsummer bloom and may obscure your view. On the other hand, its foliage is excellent for dried flower arrangements, so cut it back at will.

It's planting time now for the hellebores or Lenten Rose if you would like it to provide you with a good crop of flowers in winter. Put these perennials in a semi-shaded position under trees or shrubs, and they will naturalize there quite happily. Their pink-purple blooms will be a welcome antidote to the snow and winter cold. The colours will be all the more intense if the plants have the right conditions. The soil should be chalky, full of humus and moist, so add some ground limestone when you first plant them out.

Long-lived canary grass (above) produces flowers with a light green to reddish tinge in July.

Pond lilies (centre) liven up any garden pond.

The intense scent of lavender (left) makes it an ideal source of perfume. It also helps keep aphids away from neighbouring plants such as roses.

Water is an essential element for any plant, so now in the hottest season of the year, there are a few ground rules to follow. And if you happen to have own well, you can even leave your garden hose in the shed.

SPRINKLING AND WATERING

The month of July generally brings plenty of sun for your plants, but little rain. More than in any other month, the health and appearance of your garden will depend on the top-ups of water that you provide. Wells, taps, rainwater tanks, hoses, lawn sprinklers and watering cans all play a major role in this gardening month.

Precipitation is not the only source of life-giving water. Soil humidity comes to some extent from groundwater that is stored in pores, cracks and crevices in the ground below the water table. The depth of groundwater varies according to location, and the volume is also prone to fluctuation which is partly seasonal in nature. If it comes up too close to the surface, many vegetables will become too wet. If it runs too deep down in the soil, even gardeners who put a lot of effort into watering will only achieve modest results.

Vegetables, for instance, need a layer of soil at least 7 cm (3 in) deep that is free of groundwater, while trees with their deeper roots thrive best if the water-bearing layer is at least 1.5 metres (5 ft) below the earth's surface. In most locations that is the case and you can cultivate the usual mix of plants in your garden without concern.

Watering fills the gaps created by too little moisture from above and below. Dry spells can necessitate quite a lot of watering during the hottest part of the summer.

It tends to rain less in summer than in other seasons, yet that is the time when the garden most needs water. The water table can drops by up to 2 metres (6 ft) in the hot months, so there is a real danger of plants drying out. If the water table rises a bit it will do less damage, as plants can withstand temporary wet conditions better than a prolonged drought.

To prevent such a drought, there is always tap water to fill your cans, sprinklers and hoses. Watering cans allow you to use stored water collected in rainwater tanks or from wells not connected to the house. A pump system can make the use of colleted water even easier if you find yourself working with high volumes. Even water collected from a balcony can be useful for small jobs. Whether you use tap water or rainwater often depends on how you plan to distribute it. Money also plays a part, as well. Tap water can be expensive, whereas water collected from the roof of your house is free. However, there is more to think about than the method of irrigation. Rainwater is not always of the highest quality. If your garden lies in an area affected by heavy pollution, you shouldn't collect extra rainwater for garden watering. The quality is only likely to be acceptable after very heavy, cleansing showers. Tap water, on the other hand, can be too cold for sensitive plants in the height of summer. One thing you can do is fill drums or barrels and wait until it reaches a suitable temperature.

Well water is almost always suitable for your garden. Though it also comes from precipitation, it is channelled through underground waterways and, by the time it reaches the groundwater, has been very well filtered, so it is unlikely to pose any threat to your plants. A danger is only really presented if the channel of underground water passes through nearby rubbish dumps or historically contaminated ground.

You will be able to get a more reliable picture of this by arranging to have a well installed on your property by an expert. A well is also an attractive design element in a garden, as water is always a positive influence, whether in the form of a stream, a pond or a gentle waterfall.

In spite of pollution, rainwater is still the best kind of water for your garden. A valve you can close (above) allows water to flow from a down pipe to a storage drum.

Drums offer a simple method of catching rainwater. To ensure no wildlife inadvertently falls inside, cover the drums with wire mesh lids (left).

95

WEEDS AND PLANT DISEASES

Nature certainly provides for us, but we don't always pay it due consideration. As a result, it tends to take its revenge—and nowhere is this more obvious than in the garden. The result is not usually as drastic as this dead tree would suggest, but the increased vulnerability of plants to disease can certainly be attributed to damaging environmental influences.

This means that you should only use water that has been gathered in drums and other containers once any impurities have settled to the bottom. If you happen to live very close to a cement factory, you should even have the pH level of your water tested before you use it on any lime-sensitive plants. It is best to avoid cement-based containers for collecting water for the same reason, as they give off a certain level of lime themselves. Plastic or wooden tubs are preferable.

Acid rain, air pollution and contamination caused by emissions inflict lasting damage not only on trees, but also on other plants, animals and of course human beings.

We have already touched upon the drawbacks of using rainwater in some areas. The kind of clean, lime-free hydration required by our flowers is nowhere to be had from the skies above. Everything thrown up into the air by cars, domestic chimneys and factories as particles is carried back down to earth by the rain. This sometimes affects plants, if the fall-out is severe enough. Even when it dries, the sediment will build up on roofs and later travel from there to rainwater reservoirs.

You don't need to use chemical means to fight weeds—they cannot thrive underneath a thick cover of potato leaves (left) because they receive so little light.

Apart from goutweed, couch grass (below) is considered one of the most unpleasant garden weeds, due to its vigorously spreading root structure.

Opposite page:

Scab diseases are caused by fungi. Many maple varieties are prone to tar-like splodges on the upper side of their leaves (above right). These blotches are caused by scab.

So-called gum bleed (below right), which particularly affects fruit trees, can have many origins, e.g. waterlogged soil or lack of nutrients.

Environmental pollutants affect plants' resistance to disease in different ways. They make some plants more susceptible to fungal infections. Scab, for instance, infects fruit trees in particular, damaging both the leaves and the fruit. It manifests itself as dark splodges on the leaves, or brown and black scabs on the fruit. Maple and other decorative deciduous trees may also be affected. Collect any fallen leaves that are affected and dispose of them in your rubbish bin. There are various sprays on the market to treat fruit scab.

Annoyingly, precisely the kinds of wildflowers that are unwelcome in our gardens are the most resistant to such environmental damage: dandelion, buttercups, goutweed, gallant soldier and stinging nettle. To some lawn enthusiasts, the Bellis daisy is also a weed.

All gardeners have one particular enemy, which we want to take a closer look at—couch grass. This invasive little plant is also called twitch grass or quick grass due to the fact that it forms enormous underground root structures at an alarming rate and can only be eradicated if you kill every last piece. Otherwise the remaining roots will shoot back up again. So how can you make sure you eliminate it all, when couch grass doesn't just grow above but also deep below the ground? The only thing for it is to dig up and pull out as much of it as you can.

Despite its negative image, there is another, more positive aspect to couch grass. Because it forms such complex root networks that cover large areas, it is well suited to the task of stabilising sand dunes and preventing erosion. Its weed stock also contains essential oils that can be used to treat all kinds of kidney and bladder infections.

BERRY TIME

The last strawberries will now be beckoning with all their accumulated sweetness, and their successors on the berry canes will follow hot on their heels. Sun-drenched raspberries and uncomplicated redcurrants and gooseberries form a fruity trio that give a great deal of pleasure to small garden owners, in particular.

Your sun-loving raspberries will bear fruit for four weeks, so you can and should pick them almost daily—otherwise the fruit will become overripe while still on the vine and squash when you touch it. When you bring the fruit inside, immerse it in cool water so that any fruit worms or beetles are rinsed off. Just after you have finished harvesting the canes, cut them right back to just above ground level. Keep about ten of the young shoots per metre (yard) along with year-old raspberry cane, which will bear next year's crop.

Raspberry canes only last about two years as a rule and usually only bear fruit in their second year. If you keep them any longer, you will occasionally find the odd small berry, but you won't get another crop in the real sense of the word. For the young shoots destined to bear next year's crop, make sure the soil is nice and loose and apply plenty of mulch made of leaves, needles, manure or similar things to cover the new shoots.

Training your raspberry canes is worthwhile too. Stretch some wire between two posts at heights of 150, 120 and 80 cm (5 ft, 4 ft and $2^{1}/_{2}$ feet). Then tie the canes to the wire with some raffia. This will pay dividends at harvest time, as the espalier effect allows the maximum amount of sun onto the canes bearing the fruit. You will find they also stand at a particularly picker-friendly height, making the berries easier to extract from their prickly branches.

July is berry season. The best sign that the height of summer is upon us is the ripening of the much-loved raspberry, red and black-currants and gooseberries—whether for popping in your mouth whole or making into jams and jellies that can conjure up the memory of summer right through the winter.

Strawberry picking season is coming to an end. If you want to cultivate the plants for another year, now is the time to remove the runners from the larger plants and plant them in another bed, if desired. Then you should weed the plants well, loosen up the soil again and add some mineral-rich, organic compost. Cut off any leaves affected by grey mould or other diseases and the plants will form new shoots.

Many gardeners choose to grow currants for both decorative and edible purposes, as they are uncomplicated plants and give up delicious red, white, or black berries with an intense flavour. Some people even grow these berries as a handy form of edible hedge.

priate name, given that its berries are a bit larger and thicker-skinned.

One of the reasons for the popularity of currants is that they are relatively easy to grow. They are winter hardy and will grow in practically any soil, though they prefer a slightly loamy, sandy soil with good humus. Their shallow roots do need plenty of moisture, so semi-shady positions and occasional watering are recommended. You should prune older canes that have not borne much fruit down to ground level to encourage strong growth.

Third in the trio of high summer delicacies is the easy-to-grow gooseberry. Larger in size than currants and able to be picked from the very sour to the very sweet stage, they taste great with or without whipped cream, raw or stewed, in and on cakes or as jam. Sometimes gooseberry bushes have such a heavy crop that it is advisable to pick some berries that are not quite ripe, as well. They can be preserved while you give the others space and time to grow even tastier.

Red and white currants have a milder taste than blackcurrants, which have a slight tartness to them and contain plenty of vitamin C. They are all ideal for making jams, jellies and juice. Redcurrants are the sort predominantly used for culinary purposes because of their vibrant red colour and sweeter flavour. Some popular varieties include 'Rovada' and 'Heros', while the black 'Goliath' variety has a particularly appro-

It is thought that gooseberries were first cultivated back in the Middle Ages. The tasty berries now come in a wide range of different varieties and flavours.

Currants from your own garden are excellent for turning into jams and jellies.

AUGUST

Always turned with its face to the sun, the sunflower is a powerful symbol in some American Indian cultures. This plant comes from the western USA, where it grows wild over vast expanses of prairie. Though they are primarily used now as animal fodder and for their oil, sunflowers are still a classic symbol of high summer.

PREPARATIONS FOR NEXT YEAR

The results you enjoy now are your just deserts for all the effort you have invested in your garden in the past few months. Your summer harvest will be at its peak. At the same time, it's worthwhile to start to think about the next year, so that the fruits of your labour will not be a one-year wonder.

They look like raspberries, only much darker, but taste quite different—blackberries. In the eyes of some, they are nothing for a gardener to worry about. Blackberries grow everywhere and about the only thing you have to watch out for is that they don't take over your entire garden. That sort of attitude is all right if you don't particularly care what kind of crop you get, but if you neglect them completely, the large bushes will produce far fewer flowers and berries and if you don't protect them, a good deal of your crop is likely to be gobbled up by the birds before you even get to them.

That's not a good reason to start picking them early, though. Until they start tasting good to the birds they're not ripe enough for us to enjoy, either. It's better to cover them with netting, giving the berries time to develop to full maturity. And remember, not every dark-coloured berry

means: "Pick me!" If you touch them gently you will soon work out which ones need a few more days to develop their full aroma and their unforgettable sweetness. When they are easy to part from their centres, you know the blackberries are perfectly ripe.

Sometimes, though your blackberries seem perfectly ripe, they may still taste quite bitter (though not exactly sour). If that's the case, they may be suffering from redberry mite and the whole crop will be ruined. It climbs all over the leaves and sucks on the unripe berries, making them turn prematurely ripe-looking. If you look closely, you will notice that they haven't developed the right blackness of colour.

So instead of harvesting your crop, you now have a fight on your hands. You need to cut back the affected branches and spray the bush with a biological insecticide. Wormwood tea is one such option. As this will banish the mites only temporarily, you will need to take action to prevent them coming back. A layer of mulch on and in the soil is no guarantee, but is usually successful. Once the harvest is over, you should cut the spent wood right back to ground level and only leave the one-year-old wood standing. This will allow the bush to regather its strength for next year.

As blackberry bushes are so dark, tall smiling sunflowers look very picturesque against their deep green backdrop. Sunflowers are usually grown for decorative purposes in a garden, as it takes a lot of effort to extract all the plant's edible goodness. It's quite fun picking the tasty, ripe, wedge-shaped seeds, but extraction of sunflower oil should be left to professionals with the right equipment.

Giant sunflowers fall somewhere between an edible and a decorative plant, while the carrot is clearly a versatile vegetable, its bright orange roots only becoming visible when they are pulled from the ground. You will be able to do this for months, well into autumn, depending on when you plant the seed and which type of carrot you plant. From small, rounded varieties to long, icicle-shaped ones, carrots taste as good whole as they do grated and make a hearty side dish. They even have healing properties. The carotene that gives them their bold colour is essential to human health as a source of vitamin A or Rhodopsin, the light-absorbing pigment. Carrots also contain minerals and essential oils.

When blackberries pass their peak it's time to prune the bushes. Any long, spindly canes and any wood that has produced fruit should be radically culled. If you grow the prickly variety, gloves are a good idea.

Bounty in the vegetable garden: carrots, cucumbers, brassicas, tomatoes and courgettes are just some of the produce waiting to be taken fresh from the garden to your table.

SUMMER FLOWERS AND SUMMER FRUIT

Your summer garden will be a feast for the eyes and for the taste buds at this time of year. Your own little paradise will be a mass of colourful blooms and full of ripe, tasty fruit. You might like to starting putting some aside for later, so that winter meals can remind you of the balmy days of summer.

Fuchsias and fuchsia hybrids are often combined with other bedding plants, thanks to their spectacular colours, but they are also very effective in pots and containers. This is particularly true of the most popular balcony plant of all, the pelargonium, more commonly known as the geranium.

Fuchsias are decorative almost year round as balcony or bedding plants, in window boxes, porches and front gardens. They are never more prominent than at this time of year, when their glorious colours stand out best against the dark green foliage of a garden plot or the profusion of a pot. This popular summer flower is usually grown as a shrub, which can reach large proportions if unpruned for several years. Small trees that have overwintered under cover for many seasons can reach heights of well over 2 metres (6 ft).

Originally these flowering plants with their red, pink-filled blooms came from subtropical America, where some varieties are even taller. They belong to the evening primrose family and are named after sixteenth-century physician and botanist Leonhard von Fuchs. There are now around 2000 cultivars, some of which grow in conditions far from tropical.

In the process, colourful, popular varieties like Hardy fuchsia (*F. magellanica*) have arisen. It thrives in the shade under trees, grows to a height of 1 metre (3 ft) and produces a profusion of purple and red flowers. The plant dies down above ground in winter, with just the rootstock

surviving the winter. Dwarf varieties that grow only 25 cm (10 in) tall are also available and make pretty balcony flowers. However, most fuchsias on the market are hybrids or crossbred from several types, including the trailing varieties that look great in hanging baskets. Some of the most common include 'Swingtime' or 'Pink Marshmallow', with its white and salmon-pink flowers. Fuchsias do not like direct sunlight. They are thirsty plants that grow better under eaves or canopies and in semi-shady spots. When the first frosts come, take them out of the ground, cut them back to around 10 cm (4 in) and let them overwinter in a cool cellar or a 30 to 40-cm (12–15 in) deep hollow.

freshly picked or as a sweet/sour dried fruit. They produce a full-flavoured juice and are very decorative on top of cakes. A popular brandy is also made from apricots.

The Romans weren't familiar with the tomato, which was first brought back by explorers from the New World and has ridden a wave of popularity ever since. It is an annual plant of the *Solanacae* or nightshade family, producing yellow flowers and brightly coloured fruit for much of the summer. With over 90 percent of its bulk made up of liquid, the tomato is also an abundant source of juice. Such a vast array of varieties have been devel-

Whether stem, bush, beefsteak or cherry tomatoes—once you have tasted a ripe one straight from the vine (above) you won't want to be without them in your garden ever again.

Apricots (left) were cultivated in Armenia, their country of origin, back in the third century BC.

Cranberries (below) not only produce tasty berries but are also grown as a decorative form of evergreen ground cover.

After the flower show comes the fruity part of the month. Apricots will be in their prime, peeping out of the foliage like little northern oranges. As the species originates from the warm regions of Armenia, it likes as much warmth and protection from the wind as possible. Although the apricot was spread throughout Europe in Roman times, it hasn't quite forgotten its homeland. It is a self-pollinating tree, so even stand-alone trees can bear fruit. The juicy, meaty fruits taste good

oped that there are even tomatoes suitable for growing on a balcony. Bush, cordon or cherry varieties come in endless different shapes and sizes. Unfortunately, many commercially grown varieties have lost a great deal of their flavour due to overproduction. This makes it all the more pleasurable to grow your own and enjoy the real thing. Producers are aware of this trend towards flavourless tomatoes available in shops and have begun to change their approach from one of quantity to quality.

HEDGES

No matter how beautiful a weatherboard, lattice or wrought iron construction might be, it can never rival a living hedge for marking out borders, dividing up spaces or encircling flowerbeds. It's well worth putting in the extra effort to ensure that your green or multi-coloured boundary marker looks thick and well looked after. Birds and other wildlife will thank you for it, too.

Even a short list of plants suitable for hedges gives you an impression of how many different colour and foliage affects can be created: beech and holly, barberry and rhododendron, firethorn and forsythia, box and thuja (Northern white cedar), hazelnut and hawthorn, bamboo and briar rose…

But let's get down to work. Before planting any new hedge, the soil needs to be turned over twice, with organic material applied during the second phase. Cover the first lot of exposed soil with it and once the soil has settled, distribute some well-rotted compost over the furrow and dig this in again when you begin planting. The seedlings should be placed at regular intervals in the furrow, although the distance between them will depend on your choice of plant.

What follows is a phase of patient tending for years to come. You will often hear that hedges should be left to grow undisturbed for the first few years. This is not advisable in the case of many hedging plants, as they can easily die off from below ground. You should at least prune the tops to stimulate new growth and leaf formation in the lower area of the plants. The only hedging plants you should not trim in the

Hornbeam hedges look like a green wall and have the advantage of not losing their leaves until very late in the year. The intense green of the leaves is a welcome sight in cooler months when the garden is past its prime.

first two years of growth are Northern white cedar, cypress and white beech or hornbeam.

Which plant should you choose? To some extent it's a matter of taste, but it also depends on the purpose of the hedge. If you only need a short, small dividing hedge for something like roses, lavender is one option, as it grows up to 1 metre (3 ft) high and is planted at about 40 cm (15 in) intervals. It provides the scent of summer and a decorative lilac note, but in winter this perennial is less attractive to look at. Perhaps firethorn would be preferable. It is planted at intervals of about 50 cm (18 in) and produces an evergreen hedge with decorative orange-red berries in the winter. Both of these hedges need hardly any trimming. For larger scale outer hedges grown for privacy and warding off uninvited guests, thorny plants that grow up to 2.5 metres (8 ft) tall, like the hawthorn or barberry, are ideal, as they grow very densely and are evergreen

bushes. Be careful not to cut off their beautiful yellow flowers when pruning if you want them to grow very tall.

More work, but also more easily shaped, are hedges grown from white beech. Keep the plants about 40 cm (15 in) apart or maybe a little closer. It is important to give the beech some chalky or limey soil. It is not an evergreen plant, but does not lose many leaves, presenting a relatively even, gold-brown winter coat to the world. From the second year on you will need to give your hornbeam or white beech hedge a thorough trim.

Unsurpassed in its ability to be shaped is the box hedge. The bushes are best planted at 45-cm (18-in) intervals in a very chalky soil. The dark green plant retains its foliage and tolerates shaping extremely well. You can create the most outlandish figures and sweeping arches out of it. Dwarf varieties are ideal as borders within a garden or for graveyard purposes.

Boxed hedges are an excellent means of providing structure to any garden, whether it is a vegetable plot, flower garden or orchard.

A briar rose hedge offers complete privacy and its beautiful flowers add a wonderfully decorative touch to any garden.

CONIFERS

If you want to have green in your garden all year round, plant some conifers. The term conifer means "cone-bearing" but is often applied to all plants with needle- or scale-like leaves, even those that don't produce cones. Thanks to the large selection now available, gardeners can combine the varied colours and textures to achieve their preferred look.

> Conifers are a good eye-catching or structural element in any garden and retain their deep green colour all year. Remember when planting them, though, that some types will need a lot of space as they grow over the years!

As is true for hedging plants, a small sample of the main garden conifers shows how much choice is now available: white fir and true fir, blue spruce and pines, juniper and yew, cypress and white cedar, Canadian hemlock and Douglas fir. Other forms of conifer include larches that, like the Ginkgo (or Maidenhair tree, a very unique and ancient conifer), lose their foliage in the autumn.

An important consideration when selecting conifers is whether you have the necessary space and the right soil to offer the tree, not only right away, but as it grows. Most of these trees need sunny, open positions and a particular kind of soil that is not too rich. The yew tree is one ex-

ception to the rule, as it also tolerates shade, though it still requires good soil.

The most easy-going among them is the Douglas fir, as it can also cope with a marginal or even poor soil. Even close proximity to factories does not seem to have any effect. However, like other firs and the Canadian hemlock, it will grow quite wide in its lower regions—up to 6 metres (20 ft) across—so enough said about the need for space.

Smaller conifers will tolerate a more cramped position, but not overcrowding. By all means, plant a Chinese juniper tree as a young seedling in a corner between a patio and pathway, but remember that ten years from now it will be

1.5 metres (4 ft) tall, and in 20 years 3 to 4 metres (9–13 ft) high and about 6 metres (20 ft) wide. It would be cruel to cut it back, as it needs freedom to grow. You just have to factor this into your planting scheme.

What other points should one note when planting conifers? August and September are particularly good months to plant them. The residual warmth in the soil will do the rootstock good, while the already damp and cooler air prevents them drying out. You can only put young plants into the ground that have their full rootstock intact, packed into moistened jute or sacking, as the sucking roots need to stay constantly damp and be able to absorb the nutrients contained in the packaging. For this reason it's a good idea to leave the roots to soak in a bucket for an hour before planting. This will eliminate any air that has built up in the root region while the plant was being transported, which could otherwise hinder the roots' ability to absorb water. If you soak your plant beforehand, you need only give it a light watering after planting. This is potentially very helpful, as the tree will take hold better in windy conditions if the soil is not too wet. Conifers are often on sale now in containers; they can be planted all year round in frost-free weather.

But let's take a step back. Before putting the plant into the ground, loosen the soil down to two spade depths. This will give the roots good access to lower layers of soil. The root bale goes into the ground with the sacking still on, deep enough for the packaging to just be visible around the top of the hole. Cut the sacking and spread the fabric out a little, fill in the hole with earth, then stamp the earth down firmly. Jute will not stop the roots from growing. They can pierce the cloth quite easily. Don't add any fertiliser until the plant has taken root (and then only a little), i.e. in the following spring.

Straight after planting, you must support the plant. Ram three stakes into the ground in a semicircle around the plant, then tie the stakes to the trunk with some jute strips.

These distinctive, three-pronged bracts (left) are only found on the cones of the Douglas fir.

The Sabina (below) of the cypress family is one of the junipers that have wide, sweeping branches but only grow 1 to 1.5 metres (3–4 ft) tall.

FRUIT OF EARLY AUTUMN

It's high season now for fruit tree owners, as plums, including damsons and greengages, are ready for picking. The possibilities for enjoying these stone fruits are as manifold as the sizes and shapes in which they can be found. The different plum varieties are delicious eaten as is, cooked or baked, and preserved as jam or jelly.

However much we might criticise the ancient Romans, we have them to thank for the plum being brought to the West from its Syrian-Armenian homeland. The Latin word for plum is now the name of the genus, *Prunus,* as well as the dried version, and the Damson plum derives its name from the city of Damascus in Syria. In any case, this age-old fruit has lost nothing of its freshness despite its long history.

On the contrary, there are now countless varieties of this fruit to suit every taste, and many different colours to choose from, not only in shades of red and blue, but also plums like the mirabelle and greengage that range from pale yellow to mid green. Plums vary tremendously

Plums come in literally hundreds of forms and colours and bear many names apart from their genus name of *Prunus domestica*. The little yellow mirabelle or cherry plum and the tart greengage are also part of this large family of fruit trees, the majority of which are ripe for the taking from August onwards.

in size and shape too, from the large and sweet 'Victoria' to perhaps the most classic plum, the Damson.

These deep bluish-purple, egg-shaped plums, with their characteristic groove and matt bloom on the skin when ripe (which is perfectly natural and doesn't have any affect on flavour), are choice cooking plums. The delicate flesh parts easily from the light brown, rough stone, which is, incidentally, ideal for plum spitting competitions! But every bite of a fresh plum has that indescribable mix of sweet and sour flavours that tantalizes your mouth. Even baked in the form of a luscious cake topping, plums still manage to retain a touch of the wild about them.

The cherry plum, or mirabelle, has made quite a career for itself out of its unique colour and flavour. It, too, comes from the Middle East, though its origins are slightly less ancient. The name mirabelle originally comes from the Greek and means something like "fruit acorn". Its yellow-green appearance (though there are now red varieties), much rounder shape and smaller size make it quite distinct from most plums. Mirabelles are only slightly bigger than cherries, which explains why they are known as cherry plums.

Because they are sweeter than normal plums, some bakers prefer to use Mirabelles as a cake topping. They are also a serious competitor to the 'Marjorie's Seedling' or Damson when it comes to jam making, but the purple varieties definitely have their nose in front when it comes to stewed fruit. Mirabelles from Metz

and Nancy in France are very popular on the Continent, though their soil and location preferences are much more specific than that of conventional plums. The trees will carry an abundance of fruit if you prune them correctly, and the fruit is popular with schnapps and brandy makers.

While each variety favours somewhat different conditions, plum trees generally benefit from a moist, warm, clay soil for maximum growth and fertility. Loose, well-drained and nutrient-rich soil is also important. You can compensate for having sandy soil to some extent by watering well and adding compost around the tree. This increases the chances of producing particularly sweet fruit.

It goes without saying that sunny positions will have a positive effect on the ripeness and flavour of your plums, while frosts can only harm the ripening fruit. Late frosts during the flowering period can have a particularly devastating impact on the crop.

A deep bluish-purple bloom on the skin is typical of the common German "Zwetschge", or quetsch plum.

Compared to most plums, the fruit of the Mirabelle tree is not only a different colour but also much smaller and sweeter.

SEPTEMBER

POTATO HARVEST

Your efforts in the garden all spring and summer long are about to be rewarded. Potatoes are ready for harvesting this month. If you store them properly they will retain their flavour for a long time. To be sure of getting a good crop, though, it is worthwhile to check the plants regularly for potato pests.

It's hard to believe the potato has only been with us a few hundred years. It was unknown in Western Europe until well into the sixteenth century and was not cultivated on the Continent or in the British Isles until the eighteenth century. It then took another hundred years for its nutritional benefits to be recognized. Until that time, the staple diet of Western Europeans was almost exclusively grains and cereals. There was no boiled or mashed potato, no fried potato or hot chip, no crisp or potato fritter to be had. It doesn't bear thinking about.

If Columbus had had his way, potatoes might still be unknown today, as the explorer wanted to reach India, where the rugged tubers were equally foreign. Fortunately for us, he did not encounter the people of India, but instead found his way by mistake to the people of the Andes. When the Conquistadors followed him later to Peru they soon realized they hadn't made it to India, and certainly they had no idea that the grubby fruit of the earth they discovered and took—more or less by chance—back to Europe was worth more than all their plundered gold.

It wasn't until 1585 that botanists took any notice of the potato, and people generally spurned the rugged vegetable for a long time. This may in part be because many people poisoned themselves by mistaking the green tomato-like fruit produced from the flowers of the plant as the edible part. The leaves were also cooked at first and found to be very unpleasant. The Italians were probably the first to realize that the goodness was to be found below ground. They called the truffle-like tubers *tartuffoli*, echoed in the German word, *Kartoffeln*.

Enough cultural background, let's get down to cultivation. For small gardens it's hardly worth growing potatoes, as you need a certain amount of space to achieve a reasonable crop. Today there are many varieties on the market, depending on your purpose and the desired harvest time. The relatively early cropping varieties that can be harvested now are actually the important ones, as they are suitable for storing and will keep their flavour for months. Potatoes are cultivated after the late frosts in spring, though seedlings can be set in

Spider webs beaded with early morning dew are a sign that the nights are becoming colder after the heat of the summer. But nature will make one last attempt to ward off the cold in the month of September.

the ground as early as February in rows a good 50 cm (18 in) apart, with the seedlings planted at intervals of about 40 cm (15 in). Light, sandy or sandy-loamy soil is good for potato plants. It's also important to loosen up the soil after planting. Once the tops start to wither and go yellow,

they have reached their peak and the potatoes will be ready for harvesting.

All kinds of pests have developed a taste for these tubers. While the potato wart virus has largely been contained, the potato nematode—a tiny worm about 1 mm long—can be a recurring problem. Nematodes will disappear, though, if you stop growing potatoes in the same patch for a few years.

The most famous pest of all is the attractive, yellow and black striped Colorado beetle, which according to a particularly persistent legend, was brought to Europe from America as a biological weapon during the First World War. The beetle itself is not the real problem, as the hungry, red, leaf-eating larvae do the real damage and can strip a whole crop bare. In small vegetable plots it is recommended to pick the little beasts by hand, but for larger crops you may have no choice but to use a chemical spray.

In Western European climes, September is often considered the most reliable month for long periods of fine weather. These "Indian summers" are well known for producing spectacular sunsets.

If you've planted potatoes in your vegetable garden, you can now reap the tasty rewards.

FIRST APPLES, LAST ROSES

While the last blossoms of the season still grace your flower garden, it's time to start thinking about just the right moment to pick your apples and pears. If the fruit is harvested too early or too late, not only its shape and colour, but most importantly its taste will be affected.

The September mix of fruit and flowers lends itself to verse. Keats "To Autumn" is a favourite: "Season of mists and mellow fruitfulness, / Close bosomed friend to the maturing sun; / Conspiring with him how to load and bless / With fruit the vines that round the thatch-eves run..." Fullness is the trademark of this season. It sometimes seems that apple and pear trees will break under the weight of their fruit, and many branches certainly need trimming. This is why it's important to start picking at the right time, as this will determine the size, taste, appearance and keeping qualities of the fruit. The earliest phase of the harvest is sometimes called the picking or tree-ripe stage, but the fruit will not develop its full flavour until later. Pears and apples should not be picked too early or too late. Apples or pears that are picked too soon will retaliate by shrinking, developing unattractive colouration and losing a great deal of their flavour. On the other hand, if you leave it too late, you can be left with mealy or even rotten fruit.

You will know you have got the timing right if the fruit you pick has brown pips, green apples are light green to yellow in colour and the redder varieties have developed their true colour. If you gently twist an apple that you want to pick, you can tell whether it is tree-ripe by how easily it

Hazelnuts are highly sought after by squirrels. But your garden offers delicacies not only for the wildlife in your area in September: apples and pears are now ready for the taking.

comes away from the tree. Any strong resistance means the fruit is not quite ready yet.

You have to be very careful with pears, as you don't want to damage any of the buds for the coming year. The delicate fruit is also quite easily bruised. When picking pears, don't shake or pull them down and be careful not to disturb the natural waxy sheen of their skin.

Night frosts, though seldom this time of year, will not hurt the fruit, since pears and apples happily tolerate temperatures as low as -2° C (28 °F). Simply wait until the day has warmed up and the fruit is dry before picking it. Apples are even hardier than pears in this respect.

For rest and relaxation, now take a look at your early autumn flower garden. There will be so many plants in flower, it is hard to choose which ones to signal out. Airy and elegant *Solidaster luteus* 'Lemore' certainly stands out with its golden glow, which seems appropriate to the season and can last well into October. If you're lucky enough to have any red squirrels in the garden they may come and gather some of your hazelnuts, but don't worry—they usually leave plenty behind.

The purple coneflower is also a beauty. This plant is not only decorative but also famous for its healing powers. Echinacea was used by the North American Indians as a medicine and over

the past century has come to be used in the Western world as a remedy for infections and a good boost for the immune system.

Yellow and gold marigolds and the African marigolds will still be in flower, and their tangy fragrance will fill the air with the distinctive smell of late summer. They come in a huge number of varieties and will continue blooming until the first frosts arrove. The French marigolds, which grow only 30 cm (12 in) tall, and the towering African marigolds, which can reach 90 cm (3 ft) in height, are equally popular. The 'Orange Gem' variety is another splendid example with its full blooms and vibrant colour.

Your flower garden will be ablaze with colour at this time of year. Some of the most striking late summer flowers, apart from gladioli and dahlias, are the Mediterranean beach daisy (above left), the purple coneflower (above) and the African marigold (below).

PREPARATIONS FOR WINTER

The time is ripe for taking precautions in the lead-up to the colder months to ensure your garden still has some colour, even in the depths of winter. Heather plants that go into the ground now will be particularly hardy and weather-resistant. The popular winter-flowering Erica carnea, *known as winter heath, and its big sister, the evergreen rhododendron, are particularly good choices.*

> Purple, red, silvery grey, golden yellow— heather plants appear almost all year round in a seemingly countless array of different colours. The best times of year to plant heather are either in spring or in the early autumn.

Few people want a heather-only garden, but a large area devoted to these discretely flowering plants is always attractive. Planting them among other decorative plants and shrubs doesn't do them justice, as they are often overshadowed by more strident competitors. In the company of their peers, however, they make a subtle, graceful statement in any garden. During its blooming period heather gives the area near your home a soft warm glow.

The heather in your garden may only be a distant relative of the sweeps of wild heather to be seen on moorlands. For small gardens, there are many shades of colour, as well as early and late bloomers, plus tall plants or ground covers. Wild heather, sometimes known as Scotch heather, is merely the basic form of the many cultivars and varieties now on the market. Half a dozen of them flower purple or pink in summer and autumn. They do become paler over time but always retain some of their colour.

Heather gardeners try to achieve a certain similarity to the heath landscapes from which these rugged but graceful little plants come. They tend to plant birches along paths, use junipers as accents and break up contours a little with dwarf conifers and small firs. A touch of the romantic lurks inside any heath gardener, so most try and recreate as natural a look as possible, with no sharp lines and a planting scheme artistically arranged to appear as though all the planning was nature's own.

Defined beds and borders are taboo, while hand-made mounds, white-tinged paths and sandy hollows fit in very well. The best idea is to sketch out a plan before planting a heath garden to ensure it really does look "natural". You can get inspiration from pictorial calendars or coffee-table books on heaths. This will ensure you strike the right note in your garden design.

Sun-loving heathers are not sensitive to drought or undue heat, but they don't like chalky soils. If you have only limey ground to offer, add some sand, peat and gravel to the soil where you plan to plant them to make it more suitable for heather. Don't make the area too small, as heather will form quite large carpets and are more effective when given room to spread. Arrange your splashes of colour in large patches too; otherwise the heath could end up looking quite messy or unkempt.

As you probably won't have any grazing animals around to help, your shears will have to do the trimming work for you. If you keep heather plants well cut, they will become much more vigorous and form a dense, evergreen cover with soft contours and a hardy habit. Late summer is the right time to trim, once they have finished flowering. By way of compensation, you won't have to water them, as the normal amount of rainfall for this time of year will be enough to quench their thirst.

The bell-shaped, hairy variety (*Erica teralix*) or pink flowering autumn heather (*Erica gracilis*)

mix well with common heather varieties, and every heath should include the winter-flowering heather, *Erica canera* or winter heath. It is by far the most reliable source of warm colour throughout the winter months. However, you will need to devote a special piece of land to it, as it likes a limey soil. Set between stones or on patios, this flower won't disturb the other ground-hugging plants and its colour will soften any hard lines in the surroundings.

Heather gardens produce a range of colours (above).

The many varieties of winter heath flower from December to May, while the bell-shaped cultivar (left) makes a good show between June and September.

PLANNING YOUR SPRING GARDEN

While this year's harvest is still underway, it's worthwhile doing some long-term planning for next spring. Now is the time to decide which plants will grow where and when, taking into account your observations and experiences in the current season. For gardeners, the New Year actually begins in the autumn.

Bulbs and tubers have to be put in the ground at the appropriate time—depending on whether they flower in spring, summer or autumn. The general rule is: summer flowering bulbs are planted in spring, autumn ones in high summer, and spring flowering varieties in late summer or autumn. Apart from the planting time, two other key factors are the depth and width of the hole they are planted in.

Spring planning is not an easy task, as there is so much on offer you may find it impossible to make decisions, even if this is a wonderful kind of torment. Don't worry if people laugh at your drawings. It's quite helpful to make a rough sketch of the kind of spring garden you have in mind. Some of the ground rules to keep in mind include:

● Whether or not you sketch your garden design in advance, you'll still make adjustments to it. Note down where you have planted any bulbs so you don't lose track of where they all are.

● Bear in mind the different flowering times in your plan, so you have a good dose of colour staggered throughout the season.

- Tulips are a real must. They look good everywhere: in the lawn, the rockery, the front garden or around the patio.
- Hyacinths are another top performer. These beautiful flowers need sun and company, so plant them in multiples as borders, bedding or balcony plants.
- Here is a selection of flowers that are ideal for growing wild in the lawn and under trees and shrubs: anemones, dog's tooth violet, crocuses, spring snowflakes and daffodils, snowdrops, grape hyacinths, water lily tulips, ornamental onions and Dutch iris.
- Clusters of these varieties usually show off their beautiful flowers more effectively than single bulbs. Tulips and daffodils look particularly good with pansies or forget-me-not at their feet.
- A word of advice: put small plants near the house or the front of the flower bed and bigger blooms to the back, as they are more prominent.

When buying bulbs, a good general rule of thumb to follow is this: the bigger the bulb, the greater the bloom. Make sure the bulbs are nicely smooth-skinned but firm to the touch. A little loose skin won't hurt, but tired looking bulbs are better left well alone.

Plant bulbs soon after buying, so you don't have to worry about early frosts. You can be quite secure about this in September. Spring flowering bulbs are pretty easy-care plants and will tolerate almost any soil. Choose sheltered, sunny positions and good loose soil with added compost if you want particularly showy ones, like some of the tulip and daffodil cultivars, to perform their very best. It is always worthwhile loosening up the soil so it doesn't become waterlogged, and the flowers will thank you for the addition of compost. Make sure you leave sufficient gaps between the bulbs so the plants are not competing with one another later for space and will look their best. The correct planting depth for each variety is usually indicated on the packaging.

Back to the present—now is also the time when many other plants in your garden will be in flower. Some of the most beautiful September blooms are produced by dahlias, which are also popular with butterflies in late summer.

If you want to enjoy this kind of flower display (above left) in the spring, you need to get your bulbs into the ground in September. Daffodils, for instance, are one of the most rewarding spring flowering plants (above).

Planted in May and well fed with compost, dahlias (below) will produce a delightful show in August and September.

MOUNDED AND RAISED BEDS

Even a small garden behind a terraced house can be adapted to produce astounding crops with the help of an old Chinese cultivation technique which extends the planting space without actually enlarging the garden. By forming mounds or raised beds, this simple technique will increase your surface planting area and offer a range of other benefits, as well.

Every garden soil has to be prepared before planting seeds or bedding plants, but you will only get soil exactly as you want it in a mounded or raised bed. Of course, this takes some effort, but it is well worth it.

For a mounded bed, simply pile up top soil (with or without turf) about 1.5 metres (5 ft) wide and the depth of spade for a length of 3 to 4 metres (10–13 ft), or longer if you have space, then allow it to settle or compact. You may like to pile up some of the turf clods that you dig up as part of the mound. Then spread a fine mesh wire netting at the base of the mound that overlaps the edge of the furrow, and bend it over. This helps keep rats and garden mice at bay. Now you can start working on creating the actual soil.

Mounds and raised beds are a centuries-old, tried and true method of growing vegetables well into late summer and even beyond. The chief benefits are a rise in temperature of around 5 °C (41 °F) over flat bed planting and the increase in surface area that a raised bed affords.

Put finely shredded material right at the bottom, like twigs from tree cuttings, shrub prunings, perennial stalks and other garden waste. Let it lie loosely to aerate the soil and ensure good drainage in the future bed. This forms the base for a layer of grass clods or straw. Pile up garden soil on top of this, and cover it with some wet leaves. Compost or manure comes on top of that. On the very top, replace the topsoil you dug out originally. You can secure the ends of this hunchbacked bed to prevent it from crumbling, or simply taper it off to form even more planting space.

Inside this mounded bed you end up working in all kinds of things that would otherwise be lying around the garden and now provide central heating for the soil, as they slowly generate heat when they rot away inside. You will have an optimal amount of compost, all evenly distributed, and a thick layer of topsoil to carry the

plants. If the bed lies in an east-west direction, you will also have a sunny side and a shady side for growing different kinds of vegetables.

These will only thrive if your mound doesn't dry out, which is a real risk given the extra space and height. To guard against this, a little watering furrow on the ridge of the mound is recommended, where rain and water from watering can be collected rather than running off the sides. Mulch will also help retain any moisture.

It's better to put plants rather than seeds into a freshly made mound, as they are less likely to be flushed out by rain. Once the material has settled in the second year, you can sow plants from

seed with less risk of this happening. There are no rules about what to plant, though it is a good idea to put flat vegetables like lettuces along the side and have taller ones like cauliflower at the top. Cucumbers, courgettes and tomatoes also grow really well in mounded beds.

Over time these mounded beds will sink a little as they compact, so you will have to put new ones down eventually. If you make raised beds with a wooden frame or brick walls around the sides, they will last longer. The only drawback to this method is that you lose the extra planting space afforded by the sloping sides of a mound. The great thing about any mounded or raised bed, though, is that you don't have so far to bend over when weeding them!

123

OCTOBER

ROSES AND DECIDUOUS TREES

Each season has its own special appeal—something gardeners are more acutely aware of than others. Take some time to enjoy the rich array of autumn colours in your garden, at the same time bearing in mind that there is much to be done to ensure that next spring will live up to its promise.

Every gardener has to think about tomorrow and design the future today. But there is no better time to stop and smell the roses than in the autumn, when there is still just a touch of summer in the air. As the writer Erich Kästner once said, "Aren't you going to greet the roses? / Don't make autumn pay the price / for winter not being very nice."

He was of course talking about savouring the moment, but simply stopping to smell the roses will not suffice, as these most popular of all ornamentals need to be planted if they are to

When the days are getting shorter and the leaves are changing colour, it is clear that summer has gone and the autumn has begun. This is also another of the times when there is plenty to be done in the garden.

rival all the other flowers by the following summer. Any varieties that are not frost tender should go into the ground now, while more sensitive seedlings should be held back until March (see that chapter).

Not only roses, but also other deciduous shrubs need planting at this point, as the general rule of thumb is to plant any deciduous specimens before they lose their leaves. If you put them in the ground now they will have enough time to take root properly and gain some nourishment before the first frosts freeze the soil. In the next growth period these

freshly planted specimens will then be able to devote all their energy to forming shoots and flowers. In the meantime, they will do their bit for the garden by injecting a splash of autumn colour.

What you plant and where you plant it naturally depends on personal taste, but also on factors like the kind of soil, the size of available space, any existing plants, the overall look of the garden and so on. Are you keen on flowers, picturesque shapes, fruit or privacy? Do you want the plants to stay small, grow tall, slim, wide or bushy? What kind of conditions prevail in the proposed planting spot? Once you have established these things, it's time to go and buy the rose plants. Ones with root bales are preferable, even though shrubs and trees can be planted bare-root. If you happen to have bought one without a root bale or have received one as a gift, make sure you soak it for 12 hours before planting, then cut back the roots by a third, with the cut surfaces pointing downwards. Plants with root bales also need good watering before they go in the ground.

Make the hole twice as big and deep as the rootstock or bale. For the latter, you will have to untie the bale cloth after placing the plant in the hole and then the cloth will simply rot by itself. Fill the hole with earth mixed with good compost and distribute it evenly so there is soil between all the roots. Watering while you fill the hole helps too. Stamp the earth down firmly around the rose to finish the job.

A bed of roses like this needs careful planning and planting. October is just the right time for it.

We owe the jewel-like colours of autumn leaves to the absence of chlorophyll, a vivid green substance that lets plants use sunlight to nourish themselves. The leaves of deciduous trees and shrubs contain these bright pigments all year long; their colours are hidden during the growing season so that the leaves can do their work.

FERNS, GRASSES AND THE FINAL FLOWERS

The best of the summer show is over. But if you have planned well, you won't have to do without in the last few months of the year. Many plants will thrive without much attention, especially under trees surrounded by a warm layer of leaves. Leaves mounded around the bases of plants offer protection to wildlife, so only remove them if they're really in the way.

Now the brilliant flower show is slowly receding. Ornamental grasses turn a bronze shade of gold and naked ladies try to make the most of the last rays of sunshine. Ferns and grasses will be in their element.

Here and there a naked lady can be seen peeping out where the sun penetrates the sparse foliage still gracing the trees. Be careful, because this alluring little plant is poisonous—though it has turned out to be a blessing for some people. Gout sufferers are thankful for it, as a prescription medication for acute attacks of gout is made from the alkaloid colchicin, which is derived from these plants. The debilitating pain of gout disappears overnight, and though it's a scandalous thought, in a way, the naked ladies are responsible. The sight of their graceful calyx can also act as a soothing balm in a fading autumn garden.

The aster is another flower that provides some of the last rays of colour in the garden. It does its bit, in its myriad shapes and sizes, to liven things up from spring through to autumn. The 'King George' aster or 'Michaelmas' daisy, bushy aster and heath aster are still to be seen, but they do need a sunny site—especially at this time of year when there is less and less heat in the sun's rays. These hardy perennials that accompany us so loyally through the seasons will grow as tall as 1 metre (3 ft). The cultivar 'Rudolph Goethe' boasts large, violet-blue flowers that contrast nicely with the reds and oranges of an autumn garden.

For other plants that can't hold on so long, even in their dormant state, it's time to part with the open air. They won't tolerate the frost and have to be taken out of the ground. This includes bulbs and tubers like the dahlias, which are some of the best-performing garden flowers. Cut off any dead stalks back to 10 cm (4 in), label the plant (name, colour of flower, height) and dig it out carefully with a garden fork. Then shake off the excess soil and leave the bulb to dry with the stalks facing downwards.

Make sure there is no earth left on the dry plant and store it in a flat box at about 5 °C (40 °F) in a dark, dry place. You can also pack the bulbs into dry sand, which works well if you don't have enough cool space to store them over winter.

Follow a similar procedure for begonias and gladioli. There are a few things to remember for the bulbs of the latter. If there is any sign of thrip on the plants you will have to cut away all the green shoots down to 1 cm ($^1/_2$ in) above the bulb. This will prevent the insects from overwintering on the bulbs. These unpleasant little beasts have become expert at sucking out the leaves of gladioli until air penetrates the cell structure and causes silvering of the foliage.

If the flowers start dying too, the diagnosis is clear: thrip has taken hold. Dust any affected bulbs with thrip powder, then dry them before removing the little bulblets that form around the base of the corm. These can be then be grown too, but they take two to three years to mature. Is it worth all the trouble? It's certainly worth storing the mother bulb over winter. Follow the same method as for dahlias.

A similar process is recommended for overwintering many other flowering bulbs, including begonias, ranunculus, Indian shot, spider lilies, montbretia and other freesias.

Hardly any other plant comes in so many varieties as the fern. The maidenhair (above) is one of the varieties with simply structured foliage.

Asters (left) are among the few hardy perennials that are still flowering in autumn.

CLIMBING PLANTS

If you've erected a pergola over the summer or think your house and garden walls look a little bare, you now have an opportunity to plan ahead for some climbing plants for next year. Autumn is the ideal planting time for these clever plants, as whatever goes in now will provide enjoyment by next spring.

Plants that grow up your house walls without any assistance are called root climbers or occasionally "self-clinging plants". They attach themselves to walls by means of suction rootlets. These include ivy, climbing hydrangeas and Virginia creeper. But before you decide on any plants, bear in mind that once these robust wall climbers have taken hold they can be hard to detach.

Make sure, too, that the proposed wall is in tiptop condition, as the suction rootlets will take hold in every crack and fissure, enlarging them over time. On the other hand, they do need a reasonable gripping surface, so they will struggle to establish themselves on sandy walls or white reflecting ones. Brick walls are best and their colour is enhanced by the contrasting green of the climber.

Greening your walls is only one of the advantages, as there are other benefits to climbers besides their aesthetic appeal. A climber creates a living air-conditioning unit by providing a cushion of air between the plants and the wall. Greenery also lessens the effect of temperature fluctuations, keeping the heat out in summer and retaining heat in winter.

Unlike the root climbers, twining plants need support structures onto which they can latch themselves. These fast-growing climbers include honeysuckle, hops, pipevine and mile-a-minute vine. The creepers that use special tendrils to wend their way along wires or trellises form a distinct group of their own. Some of the most common of these include clematis varieties and grapevines. The so-called spreading climbers such as blackberries and rambling roses are unable to clamber their way upwards on their own without any assistance. Their long shoots have to be tied or "woven" through a latticework or trellis support.

A few more considerations before you purchase climbers or creepers: does the proposed location suit the desired plant? Ivy, for instance, is not keen on south-facing walls; clematis varieties prefer a cool soil and likes to reach towards the sun. Heat baking

Climbing foliage is an ideal option if you have a small garden and want to add a touch of nature to your home's exterior. It creates an additional habitat for birds and butterflies, at the same time providing some noise dampening and heat insulation.

off a house wall can make rambling roses sick. Only the vines are less fussy about where they grow and will thrive almost anywhere.

We've already mentioned the danger of fissures expanding. Another potential problem associated with plants for house walls is that these plants need frequent watering (as do any plants that grow under the overhang of a roof). The walls of your house may become unpleasantly damp from all the watering, so it's a good idea to apply a waterproof coating to the lower part of the wall before you plant any climbers.

As for any plant, the idea is to dig a deep hole with well aerated soil. You should also angle the plant slightly towards the house or support structure and add plenty of compost to the soil. Keen climbers will need a good soak after the upheaval of being planted and the gardener may also appreciate a thirst quencher, as digging holes can be a strenuous task.

You will be happy with the results you get the following year, when spring brings plenty of vigorous growth. You need to have a bit more patience with trained trees, as they take time to develop their full charm. However, when the first flowering branch of an espalier fruit tree waves at you through the window, you will be more than rewarded for your patience.

Wisteria, which is descriptively called "blue rain" in German, drapes beautifully over climbing frames or pergolas (below). Ivy, by comparison, only needs a surface rough enough to latch onto in order to climb (opposite page).

PRESERVING FRUIT AND VEGETABLES

Your fruit and vegetable garden will produce a prolific crop for you to enjoy throughout the seemingly endless winter months. Despite all the modern techniques for freezing perishables, grandma's recipes for preserving them are still the best.

A varied and thriving orchard will normally produce more fruit than you can actually eat or use in a season. There are many alternatives for using or preserving your harvest, whether as stewed fruit, juice or by freezing.

The latest technical advances are not always the most advisable from a culinary perspective. The flavour of fruit, and often the texture, changes when it is deep-frozen—and certainly not for the better. Vitamins can also be destroyed in the process. The traditional, time-tested methods of preserving fruit are therefore well worth pursuing and will ensure you have as good a supply of fresh produce as you would using any of the modern techniques.

Many people are surprised to learn how much food doesn't even need to be preserved, as you can take it straight from the garden all winter long. This applies to root vegetables in particular and kale, many varieties of which only develop their full flavour after the cold of the first frosts. Brussels sprouts and parsnip, swede and leeks will survive outdoors without too many problems. It's a good idea to keep a small supply of each of these in the cellar or shed, as frost will not actually hurt the vegetables, but they will be hard to extract once the ground has frozen solid.

Some kinds of fruit and vegetables don't tolerate either storage or freezing without undergoing special treatment beforehand. Strawberries are a case in point. Any that you cannot use straight after harvesting are best made into homemade jam. Grapes are another fruit that is difficult to keep. Freezing is not an option for them, but they will maintain their freshness a little longer if they are left on their bunches.

On the other hand, many varieties of apples can be stored all winter long if you provide them with the right conditions. They should be left untouched in a cool, dark cellar for most of the time, in a flat box or on shelves. Wrapping them in newspaper also helps. This will allow you to continue eating Jonathans, for example, until the next crop has nearly ripened. Early dessert apples will only last one month at best before softening and becoming tasteless. It's worthwhile running occasional spot checks on your "fruit bar" in the cellar, as rotten fruit must be removed to prevent them from turning others the same way. Bruises are a tell-tale sign of fruit that will soon go off. Anything that no longer feels hard and crisp should be taken out of the storeroom.

Potatoes are the classic keepers among vegetables. It's particularly important to keep them in the dark at all costs, as they will otherwise

sprout. Heat is also to be avoided, but don't err too far on the cool side, as frozen potatoes are useless. The easiest way to store them is in cloth sacks or paper bags. This lets the tubers breathe, while plastic makes them sweat. Always keep the sacks closed and away from light. It has become unfashionable to bury potatoes in a hollow under earth and straw. It is quite a lot of work and puts them at risk of attack by ground pests.

Garlic and onions can be stored very effectively and for a long time in plaited strips. Let them hang freely and in a well ventilated place: cool, frost-free spaces are ideal for longer-term storage. Plaiting them is easy. Dig out the onions and leave them to dry on shelving, being very careful not to disturb the skins too much. Then you string them together by twisting a double length of string around their dry tops and simply hang up your plaited onions until needed.

Freezing fruit and vegetables is another alternative for storing them. This method is not equally suitable for all types of produce, and many seed packet these days provide first guidelines on the subject. There is a wide range of containers on the market intended just for freezing fresh fruit.

A long-established and still wonderfully effective method of storing is canning or preserving, which is particularly suitable for stewed fruit, but also allows you to enjoy home-grown beans or tomatoes in cold months.

And finally a plug for good old-fashioned netting: cabbages and pumpkins, for instance, will keep well in dry and well protected nets hung in a well ventilated place.

Preserving or bottling (above) is a tried and true method of keeping fruit to use later, for example as a quick winter dessert or a cake topping.

Excellent thirst quenchers can be made from certain types of fruit with the help of a juice extractor (left).

GRAPES

Many grape lovers still mistakenly believe that wine can only be cultivated with the help of a greenhouse or a proper vineyard. This is only true if you live in the very coldest parts of the country and have no sunny or sheltered walls on offer. Otherwise there's nothing to stop you adding a touch of vineyard flair to your garden.

Grapevines are not only useful for the fruit they bear, but also highly decorative. They add greenery to pergolas, fences and house walls, and an espaliered vine can also serve a useful purpose as a hedge.

Don't be afraid to have a go! After purchasing an outdoor variety of grape that is suitable for your particular location, place the young plants—still in their containers—into a bucket of water to soak for quite a while. Then let them drain for about an hour before planting them. As grapevines are not keen on inclement weather, the proposed location should be a wind-protected wall or very sheltered fence. When it comes to the soil grapes are more forgiving, though particularly rich soil is not the best choice, as it will stimulate too many new shoots that compete with the grapes themselves. For most gardeners this is not a crucial factor as they plant grapevines more for their decorative value than in order to reap a heavy harvest of fruit.

Good drainage, on the other hand, is very important. The side of the house is usually fine, but you still need to make sure of it. Before planting, knock the root bale out of the pot, dig out a hole with a planting trowel and place the plant in the centre. Then make sure the roots are distributed evenly around the hole. Fill it in again, pressing the soil down firmly, and give the plant plenty of water. Then finish with a layer of mulch made of well-rotted compost.

As strongly as grapes prefer water-permeable ground, they react very negatively to drought. This is why you must water your grape vines on a regular basis. The plants will then grow quickly, but they will need staking. If you plant the vines about 20 cm (8 in) away from the side of the house, tilting them slightly towards the wall, you can run a strong wire as far as you need to, attaching it with eyelet fastenings to the wall joints.

In most cases the so-called one-rod method is recommended. This means to be sure that from one core plant you have a grapevine that grows

both upwards and outwards. You can encourage this by training the shoots as they grow. The grapes will appear on the laterals. If you want to cover a very wide area, you may need to rely on two or even more plants.

Most of the work associated with grapevines has to do with pruning. This begins shortly after planting the vines, when you cut the trunk back to four eyes and stake it. When the rod begins to grow in the spring, choose the strongest shoot as the centre rod and remove all the others. Cut away any laterals that appear on the first 90 cm (3 ft) after bud burst.

Giving each plant a winter pruning in December once they have stopped growing for the year is important for their long-term well-being. Once all the leaves have fallen, cut the main rod back to the old wood, and on one-year-old plants back to about 50 cm (20 in). Shorten all the laterals back to the basal bud. In the second year, you can stimulate new growth by cutting away any flowering shoots, so that no energy-sapping fruit buds form and compete with the main rod for nutrients.

Follow a similar procedure in the third year by shortening the main rod down to about 2 metres (6 ft). The grapevines will not develop enough robustness to tolerate fruit buds until the following year, but beyond that point the laterals should still be cut back. Pruning of the laterals continues year for year, and multiple bunches should also be thinned out. One bunch of grapes every half metre (18 in) is generally sufficient. This will ensure that the plant gets enough nutrients and even in cooler climes such vines will produce tasty, relatively large-sized grapes. The size and quality of the grapes does depend on how the summer weather turns out, though. It is likely that you will quite often harvest small and frequently rather sour-tasting fruit. But for most people this is not the main point of the exercise. You will derive a good deal of pleasure from the green wall of foliage the vines provide in spring and summer and the flame-red leaves in autumn.

A grapevine draped over the side of your house is a very attractive sight that should not be underestimated. Any palatable grapes that happen to be produced in the process will be a welcome bonus.

NOVEMBER

GATHERING LEAVES

The classic autumn gardening job is now upon us: gathering leaves. The "less is more" approach applies here, too. If you remove every leaf that falls in your garden, you not only make work for yourself but also do the garden no favours. Leaf litter protects plants and insects and is an important part of any garden ecosystem.

Gloomy, rainy days in November, when the sun's rays make a rather feeble attempt to warm the air, mark the end of the seasonal gardening cycle. However, there is still plenty to be done, even if it is only the raking of leaves or the mulching of tree roots.

Free your lawn of fallen leaves, by all means, but removing all of them from underneath your trees and shrubs, flower beds and perennial borders would be ill advised. For one thing, a warming layer of leaves helps any plants remaining in the ground to withstand the winter. It also encourages soil activity that will do your plants good in the next year of growth.

Leaf blowers and vacuums have become a very controversial issue in recent years. On the one hand, they are very practical for tidying away the leaves that can get into every last corner and they help to remove leaves from inaccessible places that your rake would have no chance of reaching. However, the price of creating a tidy garden is a high. These machines pollute the air and the noise level is quite substantial. There is bound to be a compromise that can be reached

here—with both your own relative tolerances for leaves and deafening noise, and with your neighbours, as well. The best argument for using leaf blowers sparingly is to protect ground-loving wildlife, which need the leaves for cover and happily thrive underneath them until well into the frost period. Beneficial worms, mites and insects need this habitat in order to thrive. Other flora also needs protection, like algae, fungi and other tiny organisms. It is usually enough to remove the leaves that actually clutter the lawn and dispose of any leaves from diseased trees. However, healthy leaf litter is ideal for covering plants. If you don't have enough leaves, you should apply a layer of mulch, as this is ideal for protecting perennials and grasses. Healthy leaves are also a good addition to the compost heap.

Evergreen trees do need some help at this time of year. They lose a lot of moisture through evaporation and are more likely

A layer of mulch atop tree roots prevents weeds from growing directly in the root area, but mulch needs to be removed in the spring (left).

Ferns are shade lovers and add a graceful touch to any late autumn garden with their lacy green foliage (below left).

Rake up leaves on the lawn but leave them under trees and shrubs, where they are beneficial.

to die of thirst than to freeze. Rhododendrons will tolerate frost very well, for instance. Even very well developed but not completely closed buds will survive some hoarfrosts. But they must not be deprived of water in the autumn, so keep them well watered, choosing frost-free days to irrigate them. Young firs and other conifers will also enjoy a sip or two, perhaps with the addition of a little Epsom salts.

It is also high time to put roses to bed for the winter. Apart from hardy rambling roses, all varieties will need a little protection. To be on the safe side, remove any fallen leaves before making a protective mound, to prevent black spot spores from "nesting" there over winter. For the same reason, cut off any leaves that have not yet fallen and destroy them. Then build up a mound about 10 to 20 cm (4–8 in) high at the foot of each rose. Compost is suitable for this purpose but ordinary soil also does the job.

Do not use turf to mound up around your roses, whatever you do, as it will absorb water and act like a real icepack on frosty days. Higher up the plant you can build up a layer of spruce twigs— less to ward off the frosts than to keep drying winds and excessive winter sun at bay.

Tall standard roses need special treatment, as their vulnerable grafts are located below the crown of the plant. Release any young plants from their stakes and bend them gently over— on frost-free days. Cover the crown with earth and pack the roots with brushwood. For older standard roses that are no longer flexible enough for this, it is better to fill the crown area with wood shavings or straw and pack brushwood around the plant. On no account should you wrap them in plastic sheeting.

CABBAGE CROP AND FROST GERMINATORS

The garden does not have a great deal left to offer at this time, apart from a few hardy flowers. To compensate for the lack of colour, there is plenty to do in preparation for the coming year. The autumn clean up has to be completed, precautions taken against the ravages of winter, and the odd plant can even be planted on frost-free days.

Y
ou won't be all on your own in the garden this late in the year. Even after the first dustings of snow have arrived and hoarfrost has started clinging to fences and shrubs, the winter heath refuses to stop flowering. It is used to all kinds of adversity from its Alpine homeland and not very fussy about soil conditions, either. Its needle-shaped leaves are arranged in a whorl pattern, with pink or red flowers peeking cheekily through. This plant adds a welcome touch of colour to patios and balcony boxes at this time of year.

> Only the occasional flower is still visible at this time of year, so winter heath is a very welcome sight. It adds a touch of pink in the prevailing gloom at the end of the month, while in the vegetable garden it's time to start bringing in the cabbages.

Now let's move to the vegetable garden, where there is still something to be harvested. For instance, you can pick Brussels sprouts now (and right through until spring). This Mediterranean plant was tamed in antiquity and introduced to the garden as an edible. Especially in these cold days, when we need more vitamins but nature has only a few on offer, Brussels sprouts are a welcome boost. The little "roses" perch on the main stem of the plant, looking like miniature cabbages on a stalk that can reach up to 1 metre (3 ft) in height. They taste like cabbage, only more intense and, like their larger cousin, are highly tolerant of the cold. This is why gardeners often leave them to grow outdoors for a long time or even all winter. If you don't want to go without them in summer, this is a vegetable that effortlessly survives the deep-freezing process while retaining its protein and vitamins.

In fact, Brussels sprouts should be classified as early vegetables, as the plant will continue to mature even further. However, since the available supply of fresh greens has almost dried up, these little round delicacies are often grown for harvesting in November. If you cap the tops of the main shoots (which can also be eaten as vegetables) two months earlier, the plant will be encouraged to produce an abundance of sprouts by November.

The winter heath is a less surprising sight, given its hardy foliage, than the radiance of the chrysanthemum, which has been with us all year long. This flower is available in some 5,000 different cultivars for all seasons. If you're doing any November work in the garden, you're most likely to come across the Arctic daisy, which, as its name suggests, is undeterred even by polar weather conditions. As if in defiance of the cold, it can produce stems up to 30 cm (12 in) high, sporting nodding white blooms with a golden "yolk".

But that's about all there will be to treat the eye at this quiet time of year. The rest will be up to your imagination, when you bring out your frost germinating plants. This includes perennials that need a little frost and snow as impetus to start germinating. Most of them are wild perennials from mountainous regions that need the cold to get them going. Whether they are light or dark germinating plants will be written on the seed packet, which usually includes other planting tips, but here's a brief list of some popular frost germinators: yellow pheasant's eye, aquilegia, anemones, sea holly, monk's head, lady's mantle, goatsbeard, 'Jack Frost' forget-me-not, mullein, primroses, lily of the valley, mountain avens, saxifraga, foxtail lily, and globe flowers.

Brussels sprouts are only one of the large Brassica *family. Some early varieties can be harvested in September, but most are ready to eat around October/November.*

The generous blooms of the chrysanthemum will continue flowering beautifully well into November.

DRIED FLOWERS

Dried flower arrangements nostalgically hanging near rustic wooden furniture were very popular in the 1970s. Then, like everything else from that age, they were relegated to the past and considered old-fashioned. Today they are enjoying a well-earned renaissance, thanks to their inherent charm and vibrant colours.

Any flowers you intend to dry should be cut at an early stage, which means before the buds have fully opened, as the blooms will develop further and open up fully during the drying process. This is only a general rule, as there are some plants that are better cut when in full bloom. The following is a brief list of flowers suitable for drying, with the ideal cutting times.

In bud: common yarrow, stonecrop, strawflowers, pearly everlasting, carline thistle (in bud or just bloomed), golden rod, delphiniums, roses, hydrangeas (just bloomed).

Full bloom: Chinese lanterns (once the fruit fully develops), sea lavender, globe amaranth, baby's breath, pampas grass, scotch heather and carnations.

Mature flower heads: European feather grass, Chinese fountain grass, "bunny tails" and quaking grass.

The selections above demonstrate what a wonderful ensemble can be put together with a range of dried flowers. Grasses interspersed between flowers add a touch of flowering meadow to your dried arrangements,

> The strawflower is known by many names, including immortelle (a derivation of "immortal") and everlasting. Because the blossoms open even wider when dried, they should be picked early and immediately hung up to dry in a shady spot.

which are also suitable for placing in darker corners inside your home where fresh flowers could not survive.

Flowers for drying should preferably be cut in the midday sun. They are best dried at home by bundling them into small bunches (of about five) with elastics and hanging them upside down by the stems. Simply rig up a line or tie them to a coat hanger. Paper clips are ideal for fastening them to a line. Spread the bunch in such a way that the blooms or seed capsules are not touching each other. Then put the dried material into a box, placing it between layers of tissue paper. After about one week, the drying process will be complete.

There are one or two special tips worth noting. To promote the drying process, rose buds can be held above steaming water for about 20 seconds. Then blow gently on the flower buds to make them open right up and dry them in a warm place. Hydrangeas, paradoxically, dry best when they are placed in a vase with a small amount of water. The gradually dried blooms will retain their colour much longer if you do this. The same tip applies to other plants as well, like lavender and bell-shaped heather.

PLANTS IN WINTER

Potted and container plants have already received preliminary pre-winter attention back in September. Now that they have served you well for such a long time on the patio or balcony, they will have to take up their winter quarters before the frosts come. November is also the last opportunity to safeguard your bulbs.

You will need to find winter quarters for potted plants well before the first frosts come. The plants themselves are prepared for "hibernation" from early September: decreasing quantities of fertiliser and water are signals that they need to get ready for the tougher times ahead. The winter storage area should be cool, covered and frost-free at all costs.

In some locations, the first frost can arrive by late October or early November.

Though we can't influence the weather, modern forecasting allows us to predict it with some accuracy. However, there are some basic rules of thumb that have been around forever. For instance, frosts can be expected in late autumn. At the moment they will still be light and not persistent, but even this could be too much for some potted plants. No amount of wind protection that was sufficient last month will be enough now; the plant has to take up its winter quarters. A greenhouse is ideal if you have one, of course, but a conservatory will offer enough protection. Just remember to heat it sparingly and only if a persistent frost sets in. The plants need a certain degree of coolness so that they don't think spring has arrived and develop prematurely.

For the same reason, make sure the plants in your greenhouse or conservatory don't receive too much sunlight. By February, the sun develops an amazing strength and can produce a strong warming effect under glass, which can lead plants to come on as though the warmer months are already here. It's a good idea to have a space set aside for overwintering balcony or patio plants. This corner can be effectively protected with reed or straw matting that will let in sufficient half-light for the plants to survive. It's

also a good place to keep any fish that won't survive outside in your garden pond. Fish may not live through the winter if your pond is less than 1 metre (3 ft) deep. Even deeper ponds are only safe if you keep a part of them ice free, at least most of the winter, so that oxygen can penetrate the water. This is easily done by bunching up some straw and leaving it to float in the water: this will discourage ice formation. If you're going away for a few days and can't guarantee their safety, you can, if you like, keep fish in an indoor bowl until you return.

Bulbs and tubers of non-hardy plants should be taken out of the ground in October or November at the latest. Remove any stalks or stems above the ground and store the bulbs in a box over the winter. If you want to recognise them as begonias, dahlias or gladioli when spring comes, label them prior to storage.

WILD HEDGES

Even a cultivated landscape relies on nature. Gardeners who recognise this factor often try to incorporate natural features in their garden design. Wild hedges are particularly appealing as natural borders or substitutes for garden fences. They offer privacy, while providing a refuge for plenty of small wildlife.

Wild hedges don't have to look untamed, but can be as easy to care for as a hornbeam cut hedge. Wild hedges are usually more colourful then their tamer brethren, and offer many creatures, particularly birds, a miniature ecosystem.

A wild hedge sounds less orderly than it really is or needs to be. It will only look truly natural if it doesn't grow rampant and is in harmony with its surroundings. Feel free to treat wild hedges of forsythia or Cornelian cherry, rhododendron (though not in its usual role), hazelnut, sea buckthorn, wild cherry, elderberry, rowan or snowy mespilus as you would any boxed hedge or yew. This means prune where necessary, keep it as dense as you like, help it out with water when dry and stake the upright wood if it needs support.

You should not take to it with all kinds of equipment unless it becomes diseased and needs help. Otherwise rakes and, heaven forbid, leaf vacuums have no place around wild hedges, as these natural borders not only provide privacy and a picturesque frame to the garden but also offer a home to many different creatures.

Rest assured you won't attract pests to your house by leaving leaf litter thus around your hedge—on the contrary. You will be closing the gap in the feeding chain so often broken by the forces of cultivation. You will, in fact, be taking advantage of nature's own system of control for many garden pests, allowing moles to eat May

to look after the remaining plants plus any new ones you add to replace the weaker specimens.

Wild hedges certainly need a little more space than any perfectly straight and well-manicured dividing wall. You can make up for this by selecting shrubs that won't grow too big, such as flowering currant, European fly honeysuckle, cotoneaster or briar rose—all of which bear plenty of fruit and benefit the local ecosystem.

Another factor to bear in mind with wild hedges is that you shouldn't crowd them in. Leave them room to breathe, as this brings fresh air into the bushes and opens the view, while providing cover for small wildlife. At this rather bleak time of the year, viewing the cheerful activities of birds is one of the special benefits of having a wild hedge. Ecological compatibility does require a little thought. We have already mentioned that a wild hedge can't be left completely to its own devices. To encourage density near the base of the plants, for instance, occasional pruning is a must. Remember to look out for any nesting birds and wait until the young have left the nest beforehand. To be on the safe side, never reach for the pruning shears before September.

beetles, providing sustenance for spiders, bees and butterflies, letting ladybirds keep the aphids down, helping bird parents feed their young—and only intervening if things get out of hand.

Intervention can never be ruled out completely, as even the most sweeping, magnificent wild hedge is no perfect ecosystem. Pollutants know no boundaries and can harm even the most natural of habitats. The natural landscape too, is sometimes prey to illness, so wild hedges still need to have a watchful eye trained on them. If there is a danger of any diseased or sickly plant infecting others, take it out. If you hunt down the cause of the problem, you will find it easier

If the different colours of flowering shrubs are coordinated with one another, you can create an impressive wild hedge (top of opposite page).

Freely growing wild hedges offer refuge to plenty of birds. This is one way the wild hedge does its bit towards ensuring ecologically sound pest control (opposite, bottom).

Wild roses are an ideal privacy measure (above).

Wild hedges can be strategically planted even where space is at a premium (left).

DECEMBER

EVERGREEN PLANTS

The warm colours of autumn are inevitably followed by the rather monotonous tones of winter. But even now there's no need to go without colour altogether. When the garden is not covered with a decorative layer of snow, evergreen plants—some with brightly coloured berries—act as beacons of hope in the bleak season.

respite on the shortest days of the year and look very decorative covered in a layer of snow.

Evergreen broad-leaved shrubs, many of which produce brightly coloured berries, are also featured this time of year. The firethorn is the best of them all—though it is nowhere near as robust as it looks and many gardeners believe. The varieties that tolerate frost well are often afflicted with scab, while the immune cultivars are not frost hardy. However, there are some varieties like the yellow firethorn 'Soleil d'Or' ("golden sun") that are relatively resistant to both frost and disease. If they do show signs of frost, simply cut out the affected branches. This will leave you with fewer flowers and berries in the following year but the plant itself will recover.

Evergreens need plenty of water at the end of the year, as they lose a lot of moisture through the large surface area of their leaves and needles. Make sure to check on them occasionally to see that they have plenty of water and top it up if necessary on frost-free days.

Spruce boughs offer effective protection for sensitive plants. Other places where frost can wreak havoc should also be tended to. In a garden pond, for instance, a strategically placed bundle of straw can prevent ice forming and ensure enough oxygen is absorbed.

Conifers provide you with long-lasting, dense branches that are ideal for protecting roses and other sensitive plants, as well as for covering flower beds and preventing the garden pond from freezing over entirely. They also make sections of the garden green that would otherwise look rather grey and bare. Their various tones of green provide a little

Even deciduous trees will not survive the winter without some attention. Many of them will suffer if frosts are particularly severe or persistent and won't be very strong by the spring, or may even die out. Your tidiness may come back to haunt you if you have cleared away all the leaf litter, as you can't get it back once you've disposed of it. Shrubs need this kind of protection, so you may have to resort to wood chips or other mulch options.

If you've been sensible enough to leave some leaves on the ground, on the other hand, you should now stop them from flying away by adding some branches or twigs. Plants that will particularly thank you for keeping their feet dry and warm are bluebeard, mophead hydrangeas, Canary Island broom, buddleia, hibiscus, ceanothus, and moutan tree peonies.

While not much is flowering outside, you don't need to go without fresh blooms and a bit of greenery indoors. Before the Christmas tree becomes a symbol of new life in your front room, you can add an Advent wreath to your indoor décor or make a large flower arrangement in a floor vase. In Germany they have a delightful custom this time of year, which brightens up homes immeasurably. 4 December is St Barbara's Day, which is associated with the ancient custom of bringing branches into the house to bloom at Christmas. In December, the winter is so far advanced that the branches of many flowering shrubs will have already formed buds. Cut off a few "St. Barbara branches", as they are called, and place them in a vase of water. It can take a while, but you will certainly get forsythia, hazelnut, Cornelian cherry, sweet cherry (the traditional St. Barbara branch), pussy willow or winter jasmine to flower. Almond and peach tree twigs take a little longer to bloom indoors than the others.

If you leave leaves and twigs lying in early autumn, you create valuable habitats and refuges for wildlife like birds, reptiles and hedgehogs.

Good planning will ensure that the garden need not be grey and bleak in winter. Though it is less colourful than in warmer months, a garden can still be a sight for sore eyes.

FLOWERING PLANTS IN WINTER

December is not only the time to look forward to Christmas: nature still has some surprises of her own to offer. Who would expect plants to flower at this time of year? But the hellebore and the snowball are typical examples of this amazing phenomenon—and there is still some fresh produce to be had from the vegetable garden.

The Japanese snowball bush is one of few ornamental shrubs that brings deep pink colour to the garden in the winter with its bushy flowers. Other early flowering varieties of the same family like the fragrant or Birkwood viburnum won't open their buds until April or May.

Three varieties of this extremely robust flowering plant are quite at home in European gardens. There is a white cultivar that only stands out from the snow thanks to its yellow stamen, which pierce the cold like candlelight. Its darker cousin is even more impressive, with multi-layered red blooms about 5 cm (2 in) wide. In the midst of a severe frost, it looks rather unreal, but it is another welcome sign that even the harshest winter can't conquer all.

Perhaps even more surprising is the appearance of a flowering tree that normally blooms in March but is frequently known to put in an appearance around Christmas time. There are over one hundred varieties of the snowball bush and one of them insists on flowering in winter. It comes from North America and loses its leaves early in the autumn. This means that its pink blossoms are not hidden by foliage but free to exude their fragrance unimpaired.

The berries of evergreen shrubs also provide a few splashes of colour. The holly, for instance—an otherwise unruly specimen with shiny, hard leaves—suddenly looks more appealing, as it produces attractive coral-red balls clustered in groups like grapes. A popular cultivated variety, 'Golden King', has yellow-edged leaves and no competitors at this time of year—at least as far as beauty is concerned.

In the vegetable garden there is still some produce left to delight the home chef. Drumhead cabbage is ready to eat, as it will tolerate temperatures as low as -5 ℃ (25 ℉), or even lower in some cases. Chard or beet will only survive such severe frosts in a very sheltered position, where it can absorb some of the heat reflected from the side of the house. Otherwise it's time to bring them in now too.

Although a few other vegetables are slightly more robust and can be harvested right through the winter, it's better to bring a small supply in now. Otherwise you may have to wait until the frost period is over to gather them. This applies to lamb's lettuce, kale, horseradish, leeks, Brussels sprouts and salsify.

There's no lack of other gardening projects to be done, as this relatively dormant period can be used for preparatory tasks or those you were not able to manage to your satisfaction earlier. Winter is not a bad time to establish a compost heap in your garden, for example. The thermo-composter mentioned earlier cannot be homemade, but with just a little ingenuity you definitely can construct your own simple compost silo.

To do so, build a four-poster frame into which you can insert upright wooden planks, or use a wire mesh as the outer boundaries of your box and secure it firmly to the ground with stakes. In five months at the most, any soft garden waste will have been transformed into mature compost. There will be plenty to put into your compost heap in the months to come. In the early summer weeds, grass clippings and more can be put in, and autumn provides deadheads, lawn clippings and leaf litter to compost. Anything that is already well rotted can be combined with newer material to accelerate the composting process.

Weather is always important, particularly now in the context of falling temperatures. For gardeners who don't yet have one, the thermometers and weather stations now available make ideal Christmas presents. In addition to displaying the outdoor temperature some also record the humidity level and high and low point each day.

On a somewhat comic note, hellebore is also known as the "sneezing root" in German. This is not only because it blooms in winter, the time for common colds, but also because it contains saponin, a slightly poisonous irritant once used as a sneezing powder (above).

The pea-sized, bright red berries of the holly develop from September onwards and provide a striking colour contrast in winter, particularly in any snow-covered garden (left).

Looking After Your Trees

Even the smallest garden will be suitable for one tree or another. There are several times throughout the year for the planting, nurturing and pruning of these faithful denizens of the garden. The end of the year is a particularly good time to plant trees without a root bale, as the young trees and shrubs are now in their dormant stage and can be put into the ground without much risk to their health.

Trees play an important role in the myths of almost every culture. Whether it be the mistletoe to the Celts, the ash to the Teutons, or the apple tree in Christianity, trees have always been a symbol of fertility and life itself. An appreciation of cultures ancient and modern is another good reason to plant and nurture trees, shrubs and bushes in your garden. The winter months are certainly the best time to do this.

The first thing to do is think very carefully about where you want your trees or shrubs to go, as they are not something you plant very often. Once you have decided on a suitable location, start preparing the soil on frost-free days by digging out a hole of about one spade depth and 1 to 1.5 metres (3–5 ft) wide. Dig up the base of the hole again and work some manure or compost deep into the soil. The exact depth of the hole will depend on the type of tree or shrub.

A tree needs to be planted as deeply as it was before it was bundled up and brought to you. You can easily tell how far up the soil used to be by examining the trunk above the rootstock. Place the plant in the prepared trench and check to see whether more soil needs to be dug out or perhaps a little topsoil returned to the hole. Then take out the tree once again, trample down the earth at the base of the trench firmly, and ram a 4-cm (1½-in) thick pointed wooden pole into the middle of the hole. It should be tall enough to

reach up to approximately the height of the first branches on the tree.

Now place the tree back in the planting hole, carefully distributing the roots around the pole.

If any of the roots are bent or otherwise damaged, trim off the affected parts with a sharp knife or a pair of secateurs. Then shovel the top soil back in, making sure that it fills up all the spaces between the roots—shaking the trunk gently as you work will help the earth sift down into all the nooks and crannies. Once you have filled in enough soil, tread it down firmly. You must hold the young tree steady as you do this, and then tie it to the stake.

Existing trees, particularly the fruit-bearing woods, now need some work done on their bark. Spread out cloth below a tree on a frost-free day before you begin rubbing the bark with a coarse scrubbing brush. On no account should you use a brush with steel bristles, as this can damage the surface and allow pathogens to take hold. The reasoning behind brushing the bark is to remove any dead material or pests (including their eggs and larvae) so they cannot overwinter on the tree. If any wilted, curled up leaves are still hanging from the tree, remove them as well. Caterpillars of the brown-tail moth like to hide in these leaves, as does the black-veined white butterfly, which likes to feast on the new foliage in spring. It also pays to inspect any remaining fruit. They are popular hosts for the fungi that cause brown rot. To ensure you remove any traces of these pathogens, roll up the cloth at the end of the procedure and throw it away.

The right hand tools are essential for pruning branches and shrubs.

Trees are not only important as natural habitats for insects and birds, they also play host to lichen and fungus.

GARDEN EQUIPMENT

Gardening is hard work but it can be made much easier with the right tools. There is a huge range to choose from, but a basic set will be sufficient for many of the tasks you face and will lighten your workload substantially. Though looking after your tools is another task in itself, it certainly pays off.

T o begin at the beginning—the handles of garden forks and spades come with either T-shaped or D-shaped handles (or simply a long straight one), but opinions vary as to which is the preferred option. It's best to try them out yourself and see what feels right in your hands. The majority of garden forks have four prongs and are particularly good for winter use. The blade of a spade is usually 16 to 19 cm (6–7 in) wide and between 19 and 26 cm (7–10 in) high. Smaller versions are easier for some people to handle, but don't have the same capacity as standard ones.

Among the various hoes available, the rotary hoe is recommended for digging up soil or weeding, but you will also need a weeding hoe for seed drills. For close weeding in tight corners and along borders, a smaller handheld hoe is quite effective. A hand fork and trowel set is

Gardening without the right aids and tools is no fun at all and can be a real nightmare—both for the gardener and for the garden. Keeping the tool shed in order also makes the gardener's work more enjoyable from start to finish.

a must. The fork has prongs of varying length and the longer ones are better for working with deep-rooting plants.

Rakes may be made of wood or metal. The cast iron version is suitable for breaking up clods and has to be very robust, so make sure the handle is firmly mounted. Wooden rakes are good in a large garden for raking up leaves and lawn clippings.

Saws, garden knives and shears or secateurs are all good tools to have on hand for pruning and trimming. Sometimes one tool is more suitable than another and each gardener will develop their individual preferences. For tree pruning sometimes more than one implement is required. Use gardening gloves when pruning, as you often have to hold onto thorny branches and exert quite a bit of force.

The vegetable garden requires a few additional items, such as planting lines and a measuring tape or ruler, which are essential if you want to divide up your plots accurately and achieve straight rows. You

will need a watering can with a capacity of 6 to 10 litres (1–2 gallons) for watering newly planted seedlings or seeds. Anything larger will be too heavy to handle when filled! Even adjustable hoses sometimes develop too much pressure, but you will need a hose for larger watering jobs. Make sure the material the hose is made of will be able to withstand any frosts and is robust enough for your needs.

You won't get far without buckets either, and you may need several. You will also need a sturdy wheelbarrow for carting around many loads of earth, boxes, containers, cuttings, compost, mulch and much more.

It's important to look after all your garden equipment. They need to be cleaned, dried and oiled (as needed) after every use. It is recommended to clean all tools, as it is not only the metal parts that corrode and rust. Wood will also last longer when it is well looked after.

Finally, hang your garden implements, rather than standing them upright, in a proper tool holder. This gives added protection to your spade, fork, rake and more. You will find a wide assortment of racks for hanging tools in garden or hardware shops and racks can save you space as well as lengthen the life of your equipment.

There are many different tools on the market for breaking up clods, for smaller plots as well as larger garden areas (top and centre of page).

A carefully selected range of tools makes gardening a much easier task (below left).

PROTECTING AND PRUNING FRUIT TREES

All deciduous trees, and fruit trees in particular, need some attention late in the year, as frosts and storms can take a heavy toll on them. The lack of active growth at this time of year is an opportunity for gardeners to spend some time taking precautions, looking after plants and deciding whether any need replacing.

Many useful aids that first come into their own in the winter months can be installed well ahead of time. Nesting pockets, boxes and materials for non-migratory birds will encourage them to find their way into your garden, even though some small animals may be more interested in nestling into your house. A whitewash coating on fruit trees can be applied in late autumn, but makes more sense in winter, as it will protect the trunks from frost cracks.

One of the protective measures that has proven its value is whitewashing the bark of fruit trees. This coating can be applied earlier in the season, but should not be furthered delayed now. It will prevent your fruit trees from developing frost cracks and at the same time guard against moss and lichen.

While you are working with your fruit trees, check the stakes of younger trees to make sure they will withstand any strong winds. The tie around the stake should be firm. In the case of older trees you are faced with a different kind of problem. Maybe they are past their prime. How long will your old apple or pear trees continue to deliver a good crop? Of course it's not only about the fruit. Old fruit trees have a great visual appeal, but if you can tell they are becoming increasingly barren and starting to play host to a

range of pests, the time may have come to plant some younger specimens that, in time, will replace their predecessors. If you take precautions now, you won't end up with any unsightly gaps in your garden.

In spacious orchards that are not completely fenced off and have plenty of opportunities for wildlife to enter, there is a danger that trees will suffer some damage from hungry animals looking for an easy meal while on low winter food rations. The youngest, juiciest trees are of course most at risk. If they lose too much bark, by spring they will be well on the way to an early demise. To protect them, erect some wire netting ("wire trousers") or plastic spirals around the trunks up to a height of about 1.5 metres (5 ft) to prevent them being nibbled. If you place some cuttings around the base of the trees it may prove a temporary distraction to wildlife and stop them from sampling the tree itself.

That brings us to yet another job that is worth carrying out while not much growth is occurring: thinning out and pruning. Start with the weakest looking shrubs, as the stronger ones will tolerate a haircut later in the winter. There will be plenty of days left with temperatures no lower than 4 °C (39 °F) in the last month of the year. If it is any colder you risk splitting the wood on many cuts and this will create unnecessarily large wounds.

Fruit tree pruning is something that takes practice, so it's a good idea to work with an experienced pruner the first time you tackle the job. Initially, just watch the expert at work, then gradually start following instructions as you tackle the more difficult cuts. Diseased or dead twigs and branches are the first to be removed. If there are any overlapping branches, cut out the weaker ones.

During the pruning session, do get down off the ladder from time to time and stand back and have a look at the result from a reasonable distance away. This will stop you getting too carried away and also help you identify any bits you might have missed up close. Any upright spurs growing out from the main leads should be cut away.

While container plants can be added all year round, the ideal period for planting trees and shrubs is from October to March—but of course only in frost-free ground. Larger trees, in particular, will need a sturdy stake to support them when they are first planted.

159

INDEX

PICTURE CREDITS

MEV, Augsburg: 2, 5, 6, 7, 8, 9, 11 b., 12 (9), 13 (3), 13 (6), 13 (10), 14 b., 15, 16/17, 27 t., 28/29, 30 t., 40/41, 52/53, 55 t., 63 b., 64/65, 66, 67 t., 68 l., 68 r. t., 74, 76/77, 79, 88/89, 90, 100/101, 102, 105 r. t., 107 b., 110, 112/113, 114, 115 t., 117 r. t., 118, 124/125, 126, 134, 135 b., 136/137, 139 r. b., 143, 145 t., 147 b., 148/149, 154, 155 r. b.
Silvestris Fotoservice, Kastl: 10, 11 t., 12 (7), 12 (8), 13 (1), 13 (2), 13 (4), 13 (5), 14 t., 18, 19, 20, 21, 22, 23, 24, 25, 26, 27 b. l., 27 b. r., 30 b., 31, 32, 33, 34, 35, 36, 37, 38, 39, 42, 43, 44, 45, 46, 47, 48, 49, 54, 55 b., 56, 57, 58, 59, 60, 61, 62, 63 t., 67 b., 68 r. b., 69, 70, 71, 72, 73, 75, 78, 80, 81, 82, 83, 84, 85, 86, 87, 91, 92, 93, 94, 95, 96, 97, 98, 99, 103, 104, 105 l., 105 r. b., 106, 107 t., 108, 109, 111, 115 b., 116, 117 l. t., 117 b., 119, 120, 121, 122, 123, 127, 128, 129, 130, 131, 132, 133, 135 t., 135 m., 138, 139 l. t., 139 l. b., 140, 141, 142, 144, 145 b., 146, 147 t., 150, 151, 152, 153, 155 t. l., 155 t. m., 155 t. r., 156, 157, 158, 159